How to Become

The Best Business Broker in Town

(Formerly, entitled How to Transition to a Fee Based Practice)

Second Edition

By Theodore P. Burbank, FIBBA, CBI

Parker-Nelson Publishing
17 Causeway Street
Millis, MA 02054
888-556-8118 Toll Free

Half the lies people tell me aren't true.

Yogi Berra

About the Author

Theodore P. Burbank

 Mr. Burbank is the founder of Parker-Nelson Publishing and president of Lighthouse Financial, LLC, a firm founded to specialize in providing business valuations of private and family businesses for Business Brokers and Intermediaries. In December of 2002 Ted sold The Burbank Group, Business Intermediaries, a firm he established in 1979, where he gained experience valuing and selling more than 2,000 companies. Revenues of the companies served ranged from $100,000 to $50,000,000. A pioneer in the practice of business valuations and sales, Ted is recognized nationally as an authority on the subjects.

He is a contributing author of "Handbook of Business Valuations" and "Mergers and Acquisitions Handbook for Small and Midsize Companies", both published by John Wiley & Sons. He has written seven books and five software programs on the subjects of buying, selling and financing a private business.

Ted has conducted training seminars and addressed trade groups on business transfer and valuation issues in the United States, Canada and abroad and has authored numerous articles on subjects addressing business transfers and valuations.

Credentials:
Advisory Board--Massachusetts Small Business Development Centers
Founding Director/Treasurer--New England Business Brokers Association
Charter Member and Fellow--International Association of Business Brokers
Numerous courses in Business Valuation and ongoing education in business management, finance, marketing and sales management
Professional Accreditations include:
Fellow of International Business Brokers Assoc. – FIBBA
Community Involvement:
Planning Board Chairman – 10 years, District Commissioner, Boy Scouts of America – 10 years; and other civic and charitable activities
Mr. Burbank is available for private consultations, speaking and training assignments.

www.bizBookSoftware.com,
www.BuySellBiz.com
www.LighthouseFinancial-llc.com

This work has been produced to assist fellow business brokers, and others who sell businesses to become more effective in serving their clients, their families and their communities as brokers of businesses.

The author and publisher are not qualified to render legal or accounting advice and therefore the reader should not use this writing as a substitute for competent legal or accounting advice.

Parker-Nelson Publishing
17 Causeway Street
Millis, MA 02054

ISBN 0-9645237-6-0

Acknowledgements

Many years ago, more than I care to count, I wrote the humor column for my high school magazine. It was easy writing in that readers focused on the jokes and stories involving the teachers and students and not my grammar or syntax.

Never did I ever imagine that several decades later I would be writing on a serious subject. Buying a business is a serious and life changing event that, if not done properly, can produce tragic results. It is my hope that you will focus upon the information contained in this writing and perhaps, overlook my un-sophisticated grammar and syntax.

Thousands of people, business owners, opportunity seekers, attorneys, accountants and others have contributed to the experience I gained in more than twenty years of helping people buy and sell businesses. It is they that have educated me as to the unique realities of the marketplace for small businesses and it is also they that I, unfortunately, have no way to thank.

I can thank my lovely wife for her support and encouragement and for not complaining about the many hours I spent in my "cave" (office) and not with her. I am also grateful to: Tom West of Business Brokerage Press, Concord, MA; Dr. Charles Perkins of Bizology, Inc., Chambersburg, PA; Anson Tripp of Tripp and Associates, Honolulu, Hawaii; Joe Flanagan, MBA of Old Saybrook, CT; Tam Philippi editor and proof reader extraordinaire of Woodstock, CT, Dr. Wilbur (Wil) Yegge of Naples, FL & Castine, ME for their contributions and support.

Introduction

I began my business brokerage career in 1979 when business brokerage was essentially an unknown entity in New England. I remember spending the first year or two explaining to business owners that they could sell their business even if they didn't own the real estate. What I found very interesting was the phenomenon that as soon as business owners realized their businesses could be sold they became experts in business valuations.

I learned a lot along the way, mostly by making mistakes. My business brokerage education has convinced me that no one invented the wheel. Circles are hard to make and squares are easy by comparison. I envision someone making a kind of square wheel type device and after much use, noticing the old worn ones worked much better than the new ones.

The old ones obviously worked better because the edges that impeded motion had been worn off with use. It is my belief therefore, that the wheel evolved and was not invented by anyone. Our transition to what I will call a "Fee Based Practice" was not unlike the evolution of the wheel. As I identified and rectified systemic problems, a different approach to the selling of businesses began to emerge.

I began to employ reverse engineering techniques to improve our efficiency in selling businesses. In other words, identify what is working and has worked and continue that while eliminating that which isn't working or has not worked. Sounds simple and obvious enough but isn't what is obvious the last to be noticed?

What emerged was a new way of selling businesses or so I thought. Actually, numerous people were employing similar methods to effectively sell businesses and had been doing so for many years. They referred to themselves as Intermediaries or Investment Bankers and primarily served larger businesses. What I was successful in doing was adapting the methods employed when selling larger businesses to the sale of small and mid-size businesses.

This writing is meant to assist you in eliminating the rough edges you may be experiencing in your business brokerage career.

Using the CD ROM

This disk contains Read Only Files that should be imported onto your hard drive. You therefore want to create and label a Master folder on your hard drive into which you will copy the folders from the CD ROM.

To accomplish this, access the files via Windows Explorer by highlighting your CD ROM drive. Copy the 4 sub folders from the CD-ROM into your newly created Master folder. That's all there is to it. You are now ready to customize all of the materials to your specific use.

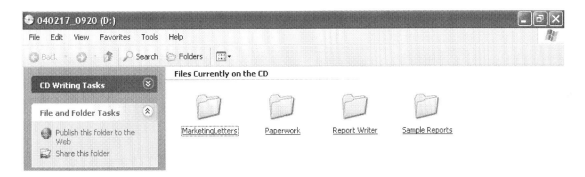

The Marketing Letters, Paperwork and Sample Reports Folders contain Word documents that can be modified or customized by you. The Report Writer folder contains an Excel workbook that is void of input numbers and is ready for you to use.

Merge Excel worksheets from the Report Writer into a Word document
Highlight the Excel content you wish to insert into your Word document. Click Copy then go to your Word document and click on Paste Special then select Picture. This action will insert the Excel worksheet into the Word page as a scaleable image. You will note that the sample reports we have included are created using this process.

I wish you well in your transition to a fee based practice.

Parker Nelson Publishing

Table of Contents

Chapter One

The Genesis
of Change

If you are presently a business broker or if you are considering entering the field then this has been written for you. Allow me to introduce myself and share a bit of my background. My name is Ted Burbank. I entered the business brokerage industry late in 1979 as one of VR Business Broker's first franchisees. Prior to that I was an insurance agent producing more than a million dollars in premiums a year.

I had spent twenty years as an insurance agent and had grown unhappy in my work and wanted a change but I didn't know what I wanted to do instead. I had narrowed the choice to finding a business of my own rather than a job. I had developed a significant list of businesses that I didn't want to be in but was not sure of what the right business opportunity was going to be for me. I found out later that my situation was not unusual and that essentially all business opportunity seekers find themselves in the same boat, that is, not knowing just what kind of business they want.

**How do you find something if you
don't know what you are looking for?**

Fortunately, for me, a former colleague telephoned that he was going to be in town and asked if we could do lunch. I quickly agreed to meet. I always admired George and still do. He is a clear thinking, hard working, giving, family man with the highest morals. My friend George had left a good paying job with full benefits and a generous retirement package in the corporate world several years earlier. He purchased a northern New England farm with an apple orchard and began a new career. The clean air and unhurried pace of country life was what he wanted for his family. Now he would be home for supper with his family instead of on a business trip somewhere. I was eager to meet because perhaps George could share with me just how he had decided upon an apple orchard, of all things, as his next career.

I mention my lunch with George because his valuable advice first helped me to find the business that was right for me, business brokerage. Later, this same advice: a) helped my staff assist more than <u>two thousand</u> business opportunity seekers find their ideal businesses b) allowed us to identify the right buyer for the businesses of our business owner clients c) assisted me in transitioning my business brokerage office to a fee based practice.

Here's what happened. After bringing each other up to date over lunch, I explained my situation and asked George if he would mind sharing the thought process that led to his buying the farm. Here is what he said.

"First you have to understand how your brain works. The brain is the most powerful organ in the human body and you have to program it to obtain the results you want." He continued, "Consider that you are a purchasing agent for NASA. Anything and everything you purchase has to conform to NASA specifications or you cannot purchase it. Correct?"

I agreed and he asked, "Do you have a list of specifications for the way your vocation will fit the way you want to live your life. Obviously my answer was No.

George explained that to program your brain to find the unknown you must describe what you are looking for. The question is not what is it? The Real Question is - WHAT WILL IT LOOK LIKE? That's where the list of specifications comes in. You have to develop a description of the business that will allow you to live the kind of life you want to live. The alternative is to live a life dictated by your job or business.

Developing your list is not as easy as you might think and, because it leads to life changing events, building your list should be taken very seriously. Don't be surprised if it takes you a week or more to come up with specifications you want to live with.

Below are examples of specifications:

Ability to build equity	Ability to travel
Family participation	Direct rather than do
Work both inside and outside	Unique business
Make own hours	Residual income
Minimal labor requirements	No inventories
Customer better off because of us	No receivables

This is a partial list. The more specific you can be the better, and omit something because it may not seem possible or practical. I took George's advice and within a month had found a business that I previously did not realize existed – business brokerage.

Much to my wife's chagrin I quit my job of twenty years and opened a business brokerage office just east of Worcester, MA. To save money I renovated the one thousand square foot store front and made the desks and partitions myself.

Initially I had six associates working with me. I kept detailed operational records and statistics to measure our operating effectiveness. I measured various ratios by associate and for the entire office.

I tracked ratios such as: Number of calls per ad, Ad calls to buyers into the office, Business tours to offer, Buyers in to offers, Offers to actual sale, Number of listings per associate, Listings to sales, and more. Perhaps my devotion to record keeping was the result of all those years in the insurance industry. In any event, it was my record keeping that would eventually be instrumental in changing my business brokerage office from strictly commission to retainer plus commission.

Here's how it happened. My wife and I were at a party and someone asked what I did for a living. Quite a few people gathered around to hear more after I explained that I sold businesses. After answering all the usual questions such as "What's the best business to buy today?" I still had an audience so I continued and pointed out that many entities sold businesses. In fact Century 21 sold more businesses than any other organization. I was quick to add that those numbers were purely a function of their size and not their effectiveness.

For example if every other Century 21 office sold one business a year that would represent several thousand sales. But, they sell less than one of twenty listings or an effectiveness rate of less than five percent. Business brokers typically will sell one in six to seven of their listings. However, (drum roll please) my office was successful in selling one in four of our listings.

The adulation and praise was short lived as on the drive home my wife asked "Is it true that you sell one of four listings?" "Why, yes indeed," I replied, my chest expanding with pride. "Yes we do!"

I was unprepared for her foundation shaking reply. "You mean to say you _only_ satisfy twenty five percent of your customers?" Oh wow! She was right. What other profession has a success rate that low? Perhaps a baseball player's batting average, but I can't think of anything else.

It's not easy being married to an intelligent woman. It took over a year for us to come up with the solution to the low effectiveness problem. Our effectiveness rate rose from twenty five percent to the high nineties percent, and now I want to share with you just how we did it.

In the modern world of business,
it is useless to be a creative original thinker
unless you can also sell what you create.
Management cannot be expected to recognize
a good idea unless it is presented to them
by a good salesman.

David M. Ogilvy

Chapter Two

Business Brokerage
Meets Wall Street

The office staff had grown to more than twenty associates and we now occupied twenty five hundred square feet of office space. This office had four interview rooms, three private offices, a conference room and a large room where we conducted seminars. The staff was divided into two divisions; Main Street, and Mergers and Acquisitions (M&A). Main Street brokers focused on smaller businesses typically with sale prices under $500,000 while the M&A division concentrated on larger companies.

From the start I had been fortunate to attract very talented people and I learned a great deal from them. John Dee joined my firm to become my Main Street division manager and a very good friend. Bob Bryant headed up the Mergers and Acquisitions (M&A) division. Both gentlemen joined my firm after VR Business Broker's "Black Friday." VR was experiencing cash flow problems and fired a lot of very talented people in their reorganization efforts.

John had been the person in charge of training and support of all VR Business Broker offices in New England. He was exceptionally talented. Bob had joined VR with the understanding that he would establish VR's M&A division. He previously managed private company M&A activities for Merrill Lynch. Together we were a unique team.

It was apparent from the very beginning that the "Wall Street" approach to selling businesses as employed by Bob Bryant was different from VR Business Broker's methods used with "Main Street" businesses.

The genesis of the two approaches to selling businesses can perhaps be best illustrated with a parable.

Many years ago two talented people decided to engage in the sale of businesses. One was located on the east coast and the other the west. Neither knew or would ever understand the other. Both were very prosperous and content in their quest for wealth, fame and happiness.

The west coast person's roots were in real estate brokerage and so he called himself a business broker. He served private companies or "Main Street" businesses and sold one business in six or seven.

The east coast broker was located on Wall Street in New York. He dealt with representatives of large Public Companies and it was comfortable for him to refer to himself as an Investment Banker. He was usually successful in assisting his client companies reach their objectives. In other words, they sold essentially everything.

Having quality representation of both approaches in my organization gave me a rare opportunity to find a way to adapt the investment banker approach effectively and appropriately with Main Street companies.

Given that the environment within which businesses are sold is truly unique, it would seem that a unique process would be the answer. Apparently modeling business brokerage after real estate brokerage was not the ideal choice. But what was the alternative?

The Wall Street Approach

The Wall Street approach is, at first, purely advisory in nature. The primary reason for this is that no one individual owns a Public company and therefore "strategic" decisions (such as selling the company) are made by a board of directors and not by individuals.

For example:
The board of directors of a large Public Company is considering selling off a particular division or a product line. This being the case, the board votes to engage their Investment Bankers to review marketplace conditions and to prepare a report of their findings.

The Investment Bankers return and present the board with their finding of marketplace conditions. The report will usually include a list of the most appropriate acquirers along with estimates and justification of prices likely to be paid by each of the targeted buyers. The report may also include summaries of market trends, recent M&A activity within the industry, outlook for the industry and recommendations for further consideration.

After reviewing the investment banker's report the board may or may not decide to sell. It is not uncommon for the sell decision to be postponed until marketplace conditions improve or other factors are addressed and rectified.

A board may decide to enhance its company's value through a program of strategic acquisition of other companies and therefore buy instead of sell. Should the board ratify the timeliness of a sell decision then the investment bankers swing into the "broker" mode. Their job is now somewhat simplified because they know who the best buyers are and how to best position their client company.

This approach makes a lot of sense. Business is business, private or public, and the issues are essentially the same albeit on different scales. How were we going to adapt the Wall Street approach to the sale of Main Street businesses?

Reverse Engineering

Our objective was to increase the percentage of listings sold. Notice our objective was not to transition to a fee based practice.

Perhaps for clues to attaining the above objective we should go to the closing table. It is always good practice to go to the end of a successful process to determine what should be in place in the beginning or as soon as possible to enhance the probability of success the next time. Engineers refer to this process as Reverse Engineering.

What we find at closing tables are sellers who are:

- Comfortable with the idea of stepping down
- In a position to sell
- Satisfied with their price and terms
- Happy with the buyer
- Confident in their broker

Also found at the closing table is a broker/intermediary who has full and complete knowledge of:

- Client motivations
- Company operations
- Competitive environment
- Market served
- Outlook for the industry

- Details of the lease
- Recast earnings and balance sheet
- Opportunity the business represents etc.

It is difficult for a sale to occur without the above in place. Would components of the "Wall Street" approach help put these elements in position and improve chances of a sale? The answer would be a resounding YES.

**Elements of the Wall Street approach
not found in the Main Street method**

- **Comprehensive client education** – Boards of directors are able to make informed decisions using current marketplace data as provided by their investment bankers.
- **Buyer Identification** – The marketplace contains many different types of buyers. The investment bankers identify those most appropriate to approach and likewise those to be avoided if a sell decision is made.
- **Values of business** – Different acquirers can be predicted to pay various prices for varying reasons. The investment banker's report delineates the probable pricing structure and justification of purchase for the various buyers.
- **Ability to consider options other than selling** – The board of directors can decide to sell, buy or do whatever they see as in the best interest of the stockholders. They are not locked into selling by signing a type of listing agreement.
- **Investment Banker (read Broker) Valued and Respected -** Investment bankers are valued as team members uniquely able to provide the "marketplace intelligence" boards of directors need to make informed and intelligent decisions.

We began developing and working on a Main Street version of the Wall Street process in order to find a way to:

1. Implement elements found in Wall Street's method yet missing from the Main Street approach
2. Make sure most, if not all, elements found at the closing table as listed above are in position before attempting a sale

"In the business world, the rearview mirror is
always clearer than the windshield."
Warren Buffett

Chapter 3

Evolution
of a Process

Private businesses are bought and sold in a very secretive if not clandestine environment. We prefer to use the word confidential. However, the end result is that an air of mystery and myth shrouds the buy-sell process.

Business Valuation

The first and most obvious area of mystery we chose to address was the value or price of a business so we purchased software that would assist us in valuing our client's business. We initially performed this service without charge.

The results were quite revealing. The reaction to the report by business owners who had already listed their business with us was negative. When we showed up with our free valuation our actions were viewed as an effort designed to reduce their price expectations. Definitely not the reaction or results we were looking for.

Reactions improved when we offered the same service, still without charge, as part of our listing presentation. Our effectiveness in selling our listings began to improve also. The primary reason for the improvement seemed to be the improved cooperation of the owners in providing us with their financials and other data.

✳ Our listing process had improved also. We developed "Business Profile" Data Collection Forms so we were sure to have a comprehensive overview of the company's operations. We also expanded our list of other information required before we could attempt to sell the business.

Custom Software

Most of the business valuation software we used and or previewed was developed for and by CPAs and not business brokers. Many of the valuation methods were inappropriate for use with small to mid-size private companies. But most of all our business owner clients found it difficult to understand and follow the valuations we were producing using this kind of software.

To solve this problem we developed our own business valuation software using valuation methods employed by buyers of small and mid-sized businesses and our database of actual business sales.

We were developing our report primarily as an educational tool for our clients, their advisors and us as well. Therefore, our reports did not just provide a number but rather a value including probable transaction structure with estimated down payment, available outside financing and the probable level of seller financing required to obtain maximum or optimum value.

Our report evolved to include an estimated all Cash Price as compared with the probable Terms Price. This dampened the "I want cash issue" and took us out of that argument simply by presenting our clients with the alternatives – Cash Price vs. Terms Price – based upon comparable sales transactions. All of our clients are business people and this approach made perfectly good sense to them. The best part was that contentious discussions which often arise between client and broker regarding a cash sale vs. terms sale were eliminated.

Surprising Results

Our proprietary database of more than one thousand actual business sales transactions allowed us to develop realistic estimates of both the probable Cash Price and Terms Price of our client's businesses. This produced interesting results. Many found they could not afford to sell as the probable cash at closing or down payment plus outside financing would not cover the existing debt (and someone's commission). Others determined the probable results of selling were not satisfactory and not in their best interests. Some decided to do something else rather than sell – perhaps just close down.

Technically business owners would have to pay our full commission if they instructed us to take the business off the market because either they couldn't afford or no longer wanted to sell for whatever reason. Why? They had signed a listing agreement with the usual refusal to sell language which triggers payment of commission. For those not familiar with the reason why refusal to sell triggers payment of a broker's commission we offer the following.

Business and real estate brokers typically work on a contingency fee basis. That is, the broker's Listing Agreement calls for the broker to be compensated only if and when the business or property is sold. Part of this agreement is a promise by the seller not to take the assignment away within the listing period. Based upon the seller's promises, the broker spends both time and money promoting the sale of the client's property. Under most Contingency Agreements the payment of commission is triggered when a seller cancels or terminates the listing agreement before its expiration.

Note provision C of the sample Listing Agreement provisions shown below. Language such as this regarding Broker's compensation is found in most Contingency Agreements.

Sample:

OWNER agrees to pay BROKER a fee in an amount equal to XXXX (XX) percent of the Proposed Purchase Price, or a minimum of $XX,XXX WHICHEVER IS MORE, immediately, if any of the following occur:

A. BROKER procures a purchaser, ready, willing and able to purchase the Business at the Proposed Purchase Price or any other offer accepted by OWNER;
   or

B. OWNER sells, leases, trades, or otherwise disposes of all or any part of the Business during the Sole and Exclusive Listing Period, regardless of whether or not BROKER was involved in or responsible for such disposition, or OWNER enters into a contract of sale, accepts a deposit;
   or

C. OWNER withdraws the Business from sale, or purports to terminate this Agreement prior to the expiration of the Sole and Exclusive Listing Period;
   or

D. OWNER fails or refuses to complete a sale, lease, trade or the disposition of all or any part of the Business after entering into a written agreement to do so;
   or

E. OWNER sells, leases, trades or otherwise disposes of all or part of the Business within ONE (1) YEAR from the termination date of this Sole and Exclusive Listing Period to any person, firm or entity referred to the Business by BROKER, or who becomes aware of the Business through the effort of BROKER during the Sole and Exclusive Listing Period.

A few who decided not to sell offered us compensation in return for our releasing them from the contract. Others avoided us and refused our phone calls. Some let us continue to try and sell their business knowing full well we were wasting our money and time. Others had their lawyers threaten us in order to make us go away.

Our willingness to provide a free work product was turning some of our clients into adversaries. This was certainly an unexpected and unwanted situation.

It's only money

Our two step approach highlighted the reality that one's motivation to sell a business is seldom money alone. The motivation to sell generally involves the desire for a life style change. Money is important but certainly not the main motivator.

As a result, an owner might accept the lower price of one type buyer in return for the quick sale this buyer would represent. The difference in dollars the owner might receive from the optimum buyer and the length of time it might take to get it vs. the amount received now from the "quick sale" buyer could result in the seller opting for the lower price. The rationale might be "It's only money." The value of time versus the value of money is a decision only the owner or seller can make. As the broker, all we can do is provide the intelligence upon which owners make the decisions that will be best for them.

Legacy vs. Cash?

Sale of the company by the piece might be preferred by owners in cases where the company owns considerable assets but has relatively low earnings. Sale of the assets alone might bring a higher price than would a sale of the business as an ongoing concern. However, if motivation is for continuation and improvement of the business an owner may opt to sell as an ongoing entity even though the liquidation price would be higher. The value of the business continuing might be more valuable and important to the owner than the additional money received from liquidation.

Quality of the Buyer and Price

What is more important to a seller, the price or the buyer? The answer is that both are usually equally important to business owners who are considering selling their businesses. There is a delicate balance and inter-dependency between the quality of the *buyer,* the *price* and the *terms* sellers may be willing to accept.

For example:
We presented two offers simultaneously to the owner of a dry cleaning plant. The first buyer offered full price with the entire price to be paid at closing. It was a straight forward cash offer with no contingencies. The second buyer offered a similar price but wanted to buy the company with no money down. The proposal requested the purchase price be paid over ten years and for payments to vary, up or down, depending upon future revenues.

Our client accepted the no money down offer and would pay our commission from his savings. What motivated him do so? Perhaps a bit of background will provide insight and understanding.

I first met my client Mitch at an American Legion Post just up the street from his business. We met in the empty lounge. The bar was closed at this time of day so a confidential conversation could be held. The room was dimly lit and we sat at a small table in a corner of the room. Fifty or so pictures of past post commanders hung on the walls.

During our meeting I asked Mitch about his motivations for considering selling. Not far from where we sat was a picture of Mitch as a past commander of the post. He pointed to his picture and said "I'm the only past commander that is still alive. I live two hundred yards from my business and my wife and I have not had a vacation since our honeymoon over forty years ago. We never go anywhere. I don't even own a car. It's time for us to live a little."

Mitch's entire world could be found between his business and his home. He could walk to everything he needed. Selling his business would allow the freedom to go, see and do those things he and his wife wanted to do, as he said, "Before we die."

Our buyer Bob had purchased several drycleaners from us over the years. Mitch knew of Bob and liked what he had done with the businesses he acquired. He didn't like the people with the cash offer and was convinced his customers wouldn't like them either. Additionally, Bob's offer requested Mitch to stay on in a supervisory role. Mitch could still be involved with his business yet not have the burden of ownership.

Mitch's prime motivation was freedom to "go, see, do" where and when he and his wife wanted. On the other hand Mitch's business was centered right in the middle of his world and to divorce him from it completely and suddenly would create a traumatic and difficult adjustment.

Mitch saw Bob as the right buyer and Bob's offer addressed Mitch's prime motivations - none of which was money.

It became brilliantly clear that in order for business owners to make informed choices they needed and wanted our two step approach to selling their businesses. They just didn't know it.

Buyer Identification

The next element of the Wall Street Approach we addressed was to identify the types of buyers active in the marketplace for small and mid-size businesses for our clients.

Sellers would always insist that:
- the "Right Buyer" would see the opportunity their business represented
- the "Right Buyer" would work wonders with their business
- the "Right Buyer" would pay their price
- they might (reluctantly) provide financing for the "Right Buyer"

Everyone knows only the "Right Buyer" pays the "Right Price." That's a fact no matter what is being sold. How to determine the "Right Buyer" other than by trial and error? If you don't know who you're looking for how will you find him? My luncheon meeting with George (chapter one) provided clues to the answer.

Four categories of buyers

Investment bankers could identify actual entities as possible acquirers for their client companies and we seldom could. Lacking the ability to be that specific we identified which of the four buyer types would most likely view the company as an attractive acquisition and why. Their probable price and terms were then compared to the price and terms the remaining buyers could be predicted to pay for the company. Our reports now included a description of the four categories of buyers active in the marketplace for small and mid-size businesses.

The business would not always be attractive to the type of buyer willing to pay the highest value and we would explain the reasons why. In those cases where the company could possibly attract the higher paying buyer we would outline the criteria that had to be met in order to do so. The criteria seldom involved increased earnings but rather operational and bookkeeping changes or clarifications.

Our clients and their advisors appreciated this insight into the marketplace and the valuable and factual information our report provided. Referrals increased as did the size and quality of the businesses we represented.

Look Before You Leap

We reached the point where we were satisfied with the value of our product/service to our client business owners. We were convinced it would be in our client's best interests to pay us a retainer in return for our services and report.

We had determined that the process of selling a business should involve two steps: Step one – purely advisory with retainer and Step two – brokerage stage with a Success Fee (commission). We had to develop agreements addressing our two step process. Chapter thirteen, and the CDROM that accompanies this book, contain several examples of documents revised for appropriate use with the two step process.

Important course change

We made the announcement at a regular Monday morning sales meeting that within twelve months we would be a fee based operation. Every listing would be accompanied by a non refundable retainer. Associates could charge a retainer or not during the interim period, However, every listing would have the report developed – fee paid or not. As you might imagine the staff's reaction was mixed. No one in our market had ever charged for listing a business.

Our staff was comprised of twenty four men and women of the highest moral character. All were "straight arrows' and "square shooters" and no one wanted to engage in anything that might be viewed as self serving. So we went through the following exercise.

I acknowledged that as brokers we had a fiduciary responsibility to our clients and that all we did would be in their best interests and not necessarily ours. To begin with, I asked for reasons why a retainer was a

good idea for us. Then I matched these answers with equally powerful
reasons why it was good for the business owner, our client.

Good for the Broker	Good for the Business Owner
Cash Flow	Commission not due if sale not timely
Have a committed seller	More committed broker
More co-operative seller	Smooth selling process

There were other reasons but the staff's biggest objection to charging
appeared to be that by charging somehow we were being selfish, self
serving money grubbers and not very nice people. This exercise illustrated
that the retainer approach was certainly a win-win situation. We were off
into uncharted waters in a state of uneasy excitement.

Complete documentation was required before the report could be produced.
That meant a file with complete financials, copy of leases, copy of notes,
employee W-2 and 1099s, etc. We actually completed a "Due Diligence
Review" of the business before the report could be produced and the
company placed "on the market". Our effectiveness in selling client
companies obtained under this process continued to increase.

How much should we charge?

Yet another Monday morning announcement - no retainer should be more
than $950. The reason given the staff was that we would continue to be
transaction driven and we did not want to become a consulting company.

That policy lasted about one month as we found that our price did not
match our prospect's perception of our services/reports value. Our price
was much too low in the majority of cases and we were actually loosing
possible clients as a result. We had to learn how to properly price our
services and that involved much trial and error before we found a solution.

Retainers that represented approximately ten percent of the estimated
commission for selling the business seemed to work best. An example: A
printing company generating two million a year in revenues might expect
to sell for between $750K to $1 million. Our commission would be between
$75K and $100K and therefore a retainer in the range of $7,500 to $10,000
would be appropriate.

By the end of our first fee based year a minimum retainer of $1,500 had evolved. Main Street businesses retainers averaged $2,500 with Middle Market company retainers ranging from $5,000 to $25,000. Most importantly, our clients and their advisors were satisfied.

Take an advisor to lunch

In order to reveal our new approach to selling businesses we instituted a "Take an Advisor to Lunch" program. We invited accountants, attorneys, bankers and anyone who advised or consulted with business owners. Much to our surprise, reaction to our presentation of our new "Two Step" approach was essentially -- "How else would you do it?" When the usual Business Broker approach was offered as comparison, the advisors' reactions were basically – "Not with my client!"

Remember, we wanted the elements that were always found at a closing table to be in place prior to our attempt to sell a client company's business. We knew our business owner clients had to meet the following criteria if a sale was ever to occur. Therefore, the major objective of the First Step was to provide information upon which an informed and intelligent decision could be made.

We wanted our clients to be:
- Comfortable with their decision to sell
- Certain they were in a position to sell
- Satisfied with their price and the terms of sale
- Happy with the buyer
- Confident in the broker

Our report had evolved to include:
- A description of the most probable type of buyer for the business and the likely transaction structure
- Recommendations, when appropriate, on how to attract the best buyer instead of the most probable buyer
- A description of the type of buyer(s) in the marketplace that should be avoided
- The best price the business might command in the current market and under what terms and conditions
- The cash price should the client choose not to provide financing

This allowed the business owners and their advisors to:

- Understand the position of the company in the marketplace and the range of value the company could command
- Choose the best buyer
- Identify the types of buyer(s) to be avoided.

Although essentially all would eventually "go to market" forty percent of our clients postponed selling based on our report.

Our clients and their advisors liked the idea of being in control of the selling process. They also valued the ability to limit their company's exposure in the market only to those who fit the profile of their chosen buyer.

Value of the process ratified

The value of our "Two Step" process to business owners would be ratified in several ways.

- We were more successful obtaining "listings" and collecting a retainer than we had been when offering our services on a contingency fee or upon success basis.
- Our effectiveness in selling our listings was also increasing dramatically, eventually settling into the high ninety percent range.
- Referrals from accountants, bankers, attorneys etc. increased significantly also.

Why were business owners more willing to pay us a retainer than they were to have us work for free? We think the one word answer is *Control*. They appreciated that our two step approach allowed them to stay in control of the selling process.

Nothing astonishes men so much as
common sense and plain dealing.

Ralph Waldo Emerson

Chapter Four

A Unique Environment

In order to fully appreciate the need for a Wall Street or Two Step approach to selling businesses we should address the unique environment in which private businesses are bought and sold. None of your lifetime experiences of buying and selling essentially anything will prepare you for what's ahead.

For Starters:
- Business owners don't want the public to know they are even considering selling.
- Business buyers will admit they really don't know what they want to buy but, as with art, they will recognize it when they see it.
- Sellers don't want to sell for too little.
- Buyers don't want to pay too much.
- Neither really knows what the business is worth. In fact, ask a dozen people and you will usually get as many different answers.

In other words, *"Don't let anyone know it's for sale but sell it for the best price to a person who doesn't know they want to buy it and do it quickly."* Perhaps this is why more than 75% of all private businesses simply sell their assets and close the doors. (1)

How Does One Sell a Business Without Anyone Knowing it is For Sale?

A successful system or process must be built upon truth and reality. It cannot be constructed upon myths or negatives. The first step is to identify and acknowledge the truths and realities surrounding the selling/buying of a private company. Let's call this foundation *Realities of the Marketplace.*

(1) More than 5,000 print shop franchisees were represented in a survey conducted by Quick Printing magazine, a magazine for commercial printers. Of the 395 franchisees that "moved on" (eight percent of the total) 76.5% went out of business whereas only 23.5% transferred ownership to someone else.

Realities of the Marketplace

All of the Principles and Methods we will be illustrating are based upon the following *Market Place Realities*:

- Motivation to buy a business is seldom money

- Motivation to sell a business is seldom money

- Different buyers pay different prices

- Only the right buyer pays the right price

- No one pays more for anything than they believe it is worth

- Neither Buyer, Seller or their advisors know what a business is worth but all have an opinion

- Different types of businesses will command different prices

- Transaction structure and financial requirements will vary depending upon the size and type of company involved

- Buyers really want "All the right things to be wrong" and not a perfect business

- No one is equally talented in all directions (No one is a "Round Ball")

- Buyers would rather start a business of their own than buy yours or mine

- It is difficult to find competent advice and counsel when buying a business

All the right things are wrong!

As previously stated, selling a business differs from selling most anything else. The conditions under which a private business is sold are unique. However, two basic principles of selling remain applicable. In real estate circles the first is referred to as *highest and best use*. The second basic principle is *motivation*.

'Whom are you?' he asked,
for he had attended business college.
George Ade

Highest and Best Use

Which has more value, a glass of water or a glass of diamonds? "The diamonds" you say? Obviously correct unless you are six days in the desert without water, then certainly, the water will have much greater value.

The one who can place a business opportunity at its highest and best use will voluntarily pay the highest price as he recognizes the optimum value. In the case of a business, the one who recognizes the *most opportunity* will pay the optimum value.

Motivation

It also has been said that a business is to its owner as a child is to its parents. The decision to sell is generally motivated by personal or lifestyle considerations. Business owners do not usually sell their business for purely financial reasons. You could say that putting one's business on the market is like giving one's child up for adoption.

The decision to buy is also a personal decision and not a purely financial one. Yes, financial considerations are an important factor but are not the driving force behind the desire to own a business.

Both the business buyer and seller are to become involved in a milestone and lifestyle changing event, one that could have very important financial implications. Suffice it to say that both will be making important decisions in a very emotionally charged atmosphere. After a sale has been consummated, neither's life will be quite the same.

Advisors will be able to assist with the financial aspects but may be totally unaware of the important personal factors involved. If one analyzes a transaction from the financial side only, it usually will not make total sense. A business is sold only when personal and financial gains are in balance. Only the seller and buyer know where that balance lies.

Let's go back to the adoption analogy. Why is it that adoptive parents do not want to adopt a mature child (you have a mature business)? From a purely logical or analytical (financial) stance, adopting a mature child makes good sense. You could choose the type of child you prefer. Perhaps a girl who enjoys hiking, fishing and camping as do you. Why not a child who has graduated from college with highest honors? Perhaps she graduated from Harvard with an MBA degree. Why not? Makes good sense doesn't it? It certainly makes good sense from a financial viewpoint. Obviously it doesn't happen that way.

Adoptive parents want the opportunity to give to the child, to sacrifice for it. They want the opportunity to shape and mold the child in their own image. The logic of adopting an older child is overridden. Even one capable of caring for you financially in your old age is seldom ever considered.

Buyers real motivation is to start a business of their own

More people start new businesses from scratch than acquire existing ones. Not very logical but it's true. What are their chances for success? Would it not make more sense to buy an established survivor?

An ever growing number of buyers are considering franchises. Franchises are very popular because the buyers gain a business they started from scratch, but they are not alone. They have help and ongoing backup.

Franchisors seldom, if ever, make earnings claims to prospective franchisees. They can get into trouble with the FTC if they do. Franchisees understand that it will take time to reach break-even and even longer before they are profitable. The buyer's prime motivation is independence - making money is secondary.

Combining "Highest and Best Use" with motivation

We have discussed two seemingly unrelated ideas: First, highest and best use; Second, personal or emotional desire to mold and shape. How can you put these dynamics to work to your advantage when attempting the sale of businesses? The answer is very straight forward.

First, what does the business need? What is not being done that should and can be done? What might be done better, added or changed?

Owners of a small business essentially wear all the hats. Business owners are in charge of everything from strategic planning to taking out the rubbish. They are responsible for it all. However, no one is equally talented in every direction. People are not "Round Balls." We are very good at some things, good at others and possibly not so good at the rest. Some things we just do not know about. Unfortunately, very often we don't know what it is that we don't know.

There are no perfect people just as there are no perfect businesses. Every business contains elements that represent an opportunity for someone to capitalize upon.

We have indicated that business opportunity seekers are not interested in solely making money! Instead, they seek opportunities to use their skills, talents and resources. They want to satisfy the desire to "show their stuff" and to be in control. If they can find the "Right Business" they want to be able to improve and make it grow. Put their mark on it. Make it theirs, and, oh yes, make money doing it.

Business owners know their business from the inside out better than anyone. However, it's the view from the outside in that is most important and is the first step in the process of determining what a business might be worth and who should buy it.

Apply "Round Ball Theory"

View your client's business from the Outside-In. You need to complete a profile of the business, (more detail on this later). Outline the strengths, weaknesses, uniqueness and areas of opportunity represented. The reverse or negative of this profile will represent the profile of the optimum or best buyer.

For example, a company makes a great widget, or provides a wonderful service. The owner is a genius in design and a stickler for quality and service. The company has grown quite nicely over the years and its product, or service, is widely used in your region.

The firm's strong suits are manufacturing and design and the weak suits are sales and marketing, administration and finance. Reverse this profile and you discover the buyer should have strengths in sales and marketing, plus a solid background in administration and finance.

When buyers possessing the required skills view the business, they will recognize the opportunities you have presented them. They also become very excited because all the right things are wrong! They can fix them. They can inject what is needed into the business. They can make it theirs. Following the adoptive child analogy, they will have the ability to send the child, (business), to college.

The person who sees the most opportunity will pay the highest price. What is more important is that they *can* and *will* capitalize on the opportunity your client has created. The company, your client, the employees, their families and yours all will win with the "Right Buyer!"

Conversely, if the business is sold or otherwise transferred to someone who fails to recognize the full opportunity:

a) your client not only fails to receive the best price, but

b) buyers are not able to capitalize upon the opportunities.

They don't know what they don't know. The future of the company and all that it serves is in jeopardy. Your ability to obtain maximum value for your client's business depends entirely upon your finding the "Right Buyer." Obviously this is equally important to the buyer.

Look at your client's business through the eyes of the different buyers in the market place. The objective is to determine to whom the business will represent the most opportunity.

"It is no use saying, 'We are doing our best.' You have got to succeed in doing what is necessary."

Sir Winston Churchill

Chapter Five

Presentation of Your Services

P erhaps the most difficult lesson we had to learn was that when business owners agreed to meet with us they weren't always stating that they wanted to sell their business. We however, didn't listen to what they were saying. We heard what we wanted to hear instead. We were sure they wanted to sell their business and agreed to meet us so we could assure them we were the best in town at selling businesses.

"I'm considering selling my business" seemed to be the most common initial statement business owners made regarding their reason for meeting with us. However, we heard "I want to sell my business." We, therefore, would begin describing the selling experience and expertise we provided. We previously stressed how our large staff was constantly interviewing buyers, that we had a large database of buyers, provided extensive advertising, etc. Business owners expect a broker's presentation to stress selling prowess and our presentations did not disappoint them.

A new presentation had to be developed stressing our ability to first help them make the sell decision and then, if appropriate, sell their business. We had to make clear that our approach to selling businesses involved two steps and was not the usual "Press hard, the third copy is yours" method.

We spent the better part of six months to perhaps a year, developing the presentation of our two step process to business owners. Mistakes were made and we learned from them. You will find some of the more basic mistakes we made outlined below. We hope you will not have to learn the hard way as we did.

Selling the Report

We were proud of our report and the work that went into creating it. It was therefore only natural that we stressed the value of our creation in our presentation. That was mistake number one. The reason - business owners want an advisor to assist them in making a complex decision and not just a report. In fact there are several organizations circulating throughout the small business community selling reports of various kinds. Few of these organizations enjoy a good reputation.

We had to learn to position ourselves as advisors and consultants rather than brokers or salespersons. Advisors and consultants do not reveal the details of how they do what they do during their presentation or pitch. Instead, they describe and stress the benefits to be derived by those who engage them. They do not reveal details until after they are hired and even then certain information is withheld.

Consider the accountant and attorney and how they present themselves. They do not attempt to educate their prospects as to the mechanics and details of their profession in order to gain a client. Instead, the benefits to be gained by retaining them are implied and stressed.

We are educators. Remember, at every closing there is an educated buyer and an educated seller. Our job is to provide the necessary education in a timely fashion.

Professional Assistance
vs. Ego Gratification

Given certain basic information regarding a business and its financial condition, an experienced business broker can usually provide an estimate of a business's value using only a pencil and the back of an envelope to do the calculations.

How much has this "back of the envelope" estimate added to the business owner's education? Have the whos, whats and whys business owners want and need in order to make informed decisions been provided or, has someone just been showing off as to how smart he is? Is the estimate correct? Should a reasonably intelligent person rely upon such an estimate or should he search out a second and certainly more professional opinion? If neither business owners nor brokers gain significant benefit from a "back of an envelope" opinion of value why provide one?

Professionals get paid for dispensing knowledge and providing information. We were convinced that the two step approach was the professional way to go. Step one of the process is advisory in nature and therefore we collect a retainer. Step two is brokering the business and we provide our services on a success fee (contingency fee) basis.

We are different

We had to stop declaring our process different from that of our competitors even though it was. There was no need to state the obvious. By so doing, we only diminished ourselves in our future client's eyes by comparing ourselves with those using approaches perceived as less than professional. Remember our "Take an Advisor to Lunch" program and the "Not with my clients" reaction of advisors to the "business broker" methods of selling businesses. The two step approach is essentially what every serious business owner considering a possible sale wants. They just don't realize it until the process is revealed to them. We learned it was best not to confuse matters by presenting irrelevant comparisons.

If our prospective client asked the difference between our methods and those of business brokers our one word explanation was *Preparation*. If further differentiation was required we would explain how other entities sold businesses – Real Estate agents, Business Brokers, Intermediaries and Investment Bankers and compare the effectiveness of these methods. Remember the story I told at a party and my wife's question on our ride home, "Are you really only satisfying 25% of your clients?" and how that led to our beginning the transition to the two step process.

He, we, I syndrome

The next lesson was to learn to avoid the ego satisfaction gained by advising clients as to what they should do. You have probably been in situations where an advisor, perhaps the attorney, begins conversation using *He* when referring to the decision maker "My client (He) wishes." After some debate the reference to the decision maker then changes to *We* or "We want." More heated discussion follows and now the reference to the decision maker changes to *I* as in "I cannot allow my client . . ." Ego can be either a positive or negative force. We must keep our ego out of the equation and help insulate our client from making harmful ego based decisions.

He, We, I is symptomatic of egos out of control. We are not players, only the buyer and seller are. It is not our business. It's not our money and it's not our life. It's theirs. We can only offer advice and counsel – not decide.

Business owners do not want someone telling them what to do. That's perhaps a primary reason they are in business for themselves in the first place. They want a travel guide to assure their safe passage through the unknown and emotionally charged process of buying or selling a business. That is, if they know that a guide is available. We had to make sure they understood we were that guide during our presentation.

The following story might help illustrate our role and the role of business owners in the process of buying and selling businesses.

Harry, a business owner, is running to an elevator and his advisor calls out for him to STOP! We are guides and as such are charged with pointing out options and situations our clients should consider before proceeding. Harry is obviously free to do whatever he wants but he has engaged his advisor to benefit from his counsel. Therefore Harry stops and reviews the situation before proceeding. From that point Harry can, should and will do whatever he deems to be in his best interests. We have done our job. Harry makes a pivotal decision with the aid of our input and we continue on our journey. It is Harry who decides whether or not to enter the elevator and not us.

In this analogy we are on the seventh floor but the elevator is on the eighth! If Harry failed to heed his advisor's words and continued without his advisor's guidance he would never know why he did not meet his objective (sell his business). Or, Harry may have decided to use the cables to descend to the ground floor as the building was on fire and all the stairwells are blocked.

To further illustrate our role as guides and not instructors consider the following event. We accompanied a friend as he visited a metal fabricator to pick up an item he had ordered. While my friend did his business I engaged in casual conversation with the man who, as it turned out, was the owner of the company. He asked me about my business. I explained that I sold metal fabricating businesses. Within minutes we were upstairs in his private office where he related his recent unpleasant encounter with a business broker. The business broker had done a lot of work including providing an "evaluation report" and a marketing package or prospectus during the 90 day listing period. What was the problem? What had the broker done wrong?

The broker had <u>told</u> him he <u>must</u> provide seller financing if he wanted to sell his business. The concept of his having to provide financing was foreign to the business owner. He had bought and sold a lot of real estate among other things and never <u>had</u> to provide the financing. His relationship with the broker soured.

The business broker worked diligently placing many ads in newspapers and on the web. He brought scores of buyers to the facility the majority of whom failed to impress the seller. The broker's listing expired and was not renewed. Both considered their association as unpleasant and unproductive and definitely not win-win. Broker and business owner parted company each convinced the other was a jerk.

We explained how the Two Step process worked. We provided him with the information and data he required to make informed decisions regarding his best buyer, best price with terms, best price on a cash basis etc. We stressed how this method put him in charge of the selling process. We left with a retainer check and the work product the business broker had provided. At the closing table a few months later we collected a success fee of $190,000.

Summary:

Position yourself as the guide through the unique selling process. It is your experience in the marketplace and your transaction expertise that business owners and their advisors need and want. Don't sell a report, don't reveal the details until hired, and finally, suppress your ego and avoid the temptation of telling clients what to do. You report. They decide.

Business owners preferred to pay us rather than have us work for free. This was evidenced by our increased success in signing new clients under the retainer system as opposed to the work for free method we used before and is still employed by real estate and business brokers.

The First Meeting

The first meeting with a potential client should be held in your office if at all possible. We give business owners the option of meeting at their or our offices but strongly suggest meeting in ours *where the walls don't have ears* and where we will not be interrupted. We find that essentially all business owners who are serious about doing something choose to meet at our office rather than theirs.

The phrase "where the walls don't have ears" says and conveys a lot. It quickly establishes that you realize the importance of confidentiality. It infers you have been involved in situations where confidentiality was breached because you met at a client's office. It positions you as a professional with an office and not someone who works from his home.

It is in the business owner's best interest to meet you away from the distractions and interruptions encountered at his place of business. Meeting at a potential client's place of business considerably reduces your chances of obtaining a client, perhaps by as much as fifty percent. So always suggest meeting at your office. It's best for both of you.

If meeting at your office is not possible then a neutral location such as a restaurant or coffee shop might serve as a second best choice. However, restaurant and coffee shop walls do have ears so choose the most private setting possible. Be sure your future client understands your concern for maintaining confidentiality.

The Meeting

When your prospective client arrives at your office, treat him as you might a guest in your home. Thank him for coming. Offer coffee, tea or a soft drink and then settle into a comfortable setting away from your desk (place of business). Avoid meeting at your desk as chance of interruption by incoming telephone calls and eager staff are very significant.

An interview room or small conference room is an ideal place to meet. Point out to your prospective client that you are meeting in a conference room to insure you are not interrupted by phone calls and staff. Meet in a conference room that does not have a telephone in it. If the room does contain a phone make sure your invitee knows you have left instructions that you are not to be disturbed or even better, unplug it.

Meeting in a conference room also allows you to keep your promise to provide an environment where walls do not have ears and where extremely confidential matters can be discussed privately.

After brief niceties are exchanged, you want to ask your guest about himself. Ask him to tell you about his business and what motivated him to visit your office. Notice it wasn't what motivates you to want to sell. You may have to address motivation several times and in different ways before you get to the real answer.

Business owners do not usually have an opportunity to talk about their business. Certainly employees, customers, vendors and competitors with whom business owners interact every day are not candidates for such conversations. Therefore, this part of the session can become lengthy. You may have to take control by asking closed questions. A closed question is one that should be answered with either a yes or no. An example: "Are you open on Sundays?"

In situations where your guest is not very talkative you may have to ask a series of open questions or questions that require amplification. An example, 'Why did you choose to locate your business in Atlanta?"

Once you determine this section of the session has been completed you volunteer to provide some information and insight into the buy/sell process. An overview of what a presentation contains follows.

Presentation Essentials

Presentations to potential sell side clients varied from one associate to another. However, all covered several essential elements. All began with the business owners talking briefly about their businesses and motivations.

Components of all presentations were:
- Brief introduction of yourself and your firm
- Overview of Unique Process illustrating why selling a business is different from selling essentially anything else

Components to be woven into the presentations included:
- Motivation to buy or sell a business is seldom money
- Different buyers pay different prices
- Only the right buyer pays the right price
- No one pays more for anything than he believes it is worth
- Neither Buyer, Seller or their advisors know what a business is worth but all have an opinion
- Buyers really want "All the right things to be wrong with the business"
- No one person is equally talented in all directions (No-one is a "Round Ball")
- Buyers really would prefer to start a business of their own rather than buy yours or mine
- Banks are reluctant to lend on goodwill (goodwill being the business value in excess of its asset value)
- Future success of the business depends on the new owner's skills

Remember, business owners want the two step approach once they understand why and that it's available to them.

Illustrate the control the two step process provides the business owner i.e. Advisory Phase first then, if appropriate (40% do not proceed immediately), the Selling Phase (either by us or by themselves).

The presentation would vary by individual but would cover all of the bases above concluded by asking "Does this make sense?" The answer was generally Yes followed by the question "How do you get paid?" If the question regarding our compensation failed to arise I personally would continue for awhile longer and close again. If there is still no reference to compensation, I would then thank them for their time, give them my card and end the session not expecting to ever hear from them again.

My reasoning for the above is that if the compensation subject was not broached or, if payment of our retainer was rejected, the prospective clients had not perceived value either because they were not serious or knew they didn't have anything of value to sell.

My thinking was ratified as being correct a couple of years later by a fellow business broker I'll call Max (not his real name). We had previously sold two businesses Max owned.   Apparently, we made it look so easy and attractive that he decided to become a business broker himself.

It seemed every time Max and I would meet at New England Business Broker's Association (NEBBA) meetings he would mention a business owner to whom we had made a presentation but he had "won" the listing. Finally, after a couple of years of this, I asked him, "Max, be straight with me. Have you ever made a dime from any of the listings you *won* from my firm?" He thought for a short while and replied, "No, I haven't."

Intermediary vs. Broker

Before we proceed further I have to stress the need to change the way you refer to yourself and your activities. No longer should you refer to yourself as a Broker. This is difficult to do but must be done. The word Broker must be eliminated from your vocabulary and from your company name if it is there.

As background for this "Not a Broker" position I offer the following tale of evolution.

I can also sell large companies

I used to conduct business as a VR Business Broker franchisee. Long before developing the two step process I noticed the difficulty we were experiencing in obtaining larger listings. The years of my flooding the classifieds business opportunity section with our ads for small Main Street businesses had effectively branded us a seller of small businesses. My extensive advertising of small businesses such as dry cleaners, coffee and pizza shops effectively located our territory and expertise on Main Street.

I found I had positioned my firm as brokers of small businesses stating "We can sell large businesses too." This was not the strong position I wanted. Our two step process allowed us to reverse the previous impression i.e. "We primarily sell larger businesses but perhaps we can handle the sale of yours." I never would state anything like that but that's how, quite by accident rather than design, we became positioned in our marketplace. Even NEBBA members would refer to us as serving "Middle market" companies even though we still sold our share of dry cleaners and restaurants.

I had changed our name and was doing business as The Burbank Group and down playing the VR association and the word broker. A couple of years later we dropped the VR franchise altogether. You may rightly ask what's wrong with referring to one's self as a broker. Isn't a broker defined as someone who sells something that belongs to another? Yes and I agree. No matter what we call ourselves we are brokers. So what is the problem?

I was to have the perceived problem explained by a group of fifteen business owners. They would explain exactly why they would not want a broker selling their business. How this came about is explained below.

Focus Group

As a member of the Small Business Association of New England, SBANE, I hosted fifteen business owners who would gather weekly at a different member's place of business. The objective was to act as a focus group for the host and address a situation, problem, or topic of the host's choosing. It was a wonderful program as it provided a unique platform where frank and open peer to peer discussions regarding subjects of interest only to business owners could occur.

I was hosting the first meeting of this group and no one knew as yet what business I was in. The sign on my door simply read 'The Burbank Group." My question to the group was, "If you were to decide to sell your business how would you go about doing so? I was not prepared for the answers.

After general discussion all agreed that they weren't quite sure. However, they were consistent in resisting the use of a broker. They may have never met a business broker, yet they knew they didn't want one selling their business. Most agreed they would "do it themselves."

Unfortunately the men and women in our focus group were reluctant to use a Business Broker, in large part due to their automatic reflex association with real estate broker methodologies.

The reasons given included: "No one understands my business the way I do." "I know the players in this industry better than anyone else." "Brokers charge too much money." "A Broker will not be able to maintain confidentiality."

Whether any of the above reasons are true, accurate, or relevant is not important. What is important is their perception of what a business broker is and does. They intuitively knew selling a business was, at the least, different than selling real estate. In fact, whatever is done to sell real estate usually should be avoided when selling a business. For example we do not use For Sale signs when selling businesses.

Business owners intuitively knew they did not want a real estate approach applied to the sale of their business but they had no knowledge of what other approaches were available. Therefore, in true entrepreneurial style, they would rather attempt the sale of their business themselves.

Perhaps you now have a better understanding of why we decided to avoid using words with any association to buying or selling real estate. The first word to go after BROKER was LISTING. We replaced it with Assignment. We no longer had listings. Instead we had assignments and Client Companies. COMMISSION was replaced next by Success Fee. UP FRONT FEES were forbidden but Retainers were terrific. Our associates worked either the Sell Side or the Buy Side and LISTING or SELLING BROKERS were history.

Making the change was hard at first. We actually thought we sounded quite odd. The staff quickly became comfortable with the new language and our effectiveness in attracting Sell Side Assignments increased.

"Do what you can, with what you have,
where you are."

Theodore Roosevelt

Chapter Six

Sample
Presentation

What follows is an example presentation of the two step process for a prospective sell side client. Essentially everything covered in the presentation has been addressed earlier in this writing. You will eventually develop your own style in presenting the benefits of the Wall Street or Two Step approach.

Your presentation should reveal the unique elements found when selling a business i.e.

Unique Elements:
- Need to maintain confidentiality or "Don't let anyone know it's for sale"
- Buyers don't know what they want to buy
- No one really knows the value of a business but everyone has an opinion
- Lenders reluctant to lend on business goodwill without outside collateral
- Major element of value (earnings) disguised
- Future value of a business is dependant upon the person who buys it

Realities:
- Motivation to buy a business is seldom money
- Motivation to sell a business is seldom money
- Different buyers pay different prices
- Only the right buyer pays the right price
- No one pays more for anything than they believe it is worth
- Neither Buyer, Seller or their advisors know what a business is worth but all have an opinion
- Different types of business will command different prices
- Transaction structure and financial requirements will vary depending upon size and type of company involved

- Buyers really want "All the right things to be wrong with the business"
  - No one is equally talented in all directions (No one is a "Round Ball")
  - Buyers would prefer to start a business of their own rather than buy yours or mine
  - It is difficult to find competent advice and counsel
  - Price and Value increase as one's perception of risk decreases
  - Price and Value diminish when financing is expensive, restricted, difficult or impossible to obtain and increase when opposite conditions prevail

Your presentation should weave the unique elements present when selling a business with the realities of life and the marketplace into a fabric that represents a comfortable solution to the problem of how to sell a business without letting anyone know it's for sale. A sample follows.

Sample Presentation:

When your prospective client has finished sharing business and motivation information it's your turn. You may proceed as follows. First *very briefly* share something about yourself and your firm. Be sure to keep this concise. Second, give an overview of the unique process of selling businesses.

"For starters you must know that the rules and environment in and under which businesses are sold are different. Yes, different than the rules and environment in which anything else you can imagine is sold. In fact your lifetime of experience in buying and selling cars, boats, houses or anything else fails to prepare you to sell or buy a business."

Examples:

Most business owners ask that we maintain utmost confidentiality. We understand confidentiality is essential as business value will be diminished or actually destroyed if and when it becomes common knowledge that it is for sale or that the owner is even considering selling.

"Business owners will also admit they really don't know what their business is worth but do know what they would like to get for it. How many answers do you think you might get if you ask twelve people what a business is worth? A common answer of business owners and others is thirteen! Nobody really knows what a business is worth but everyone has an opinion."

"What you might not realize is that most buyers do not know what they want to buy. Buyers come to us and confidently proclaim their desire to acquire a light manufacturing or distribution business. This is actually code for "I don't know what I want to buy and would feel foolish if I admitted it." They do not know what a business is worth either but know they don't want to pay too much."

"To sum up the unique environment as described so far:
Sell my business quickly without letting anyone know it is for sale. Sell it to that person who doesn't know they want to buy it. The seller will not settle for too little and the buyer will not pay too much yet neither really knows what the business is worth."

You now ask a rhetorical question "**How do you sell something without letting anyone know it is for sale?**" After a proper pause allowing the business owner time to think about the question you respond. "That's what we do best and it's how we make our living."

You continue. "Let me explain how we do it. First one cannot base a successful process upon negatives. Successful processes must be solidly rooted in truths and reality while addressing motivations. So what are these truths, realities and motivations that must be addressed?"

Money is not the primary motivation to either buy or sell a business:

When you are the business owner you can't be fired but neither can you just quit. Motivation to sell is seldom the proceeds or money from a sale. Motivation to sell typically involves the desire for a lifestyle change.

Motivation to buy a business is seldom money either. Don't get me wrong. Money is important. It's just not the primary motivator. Doing one's own thing and being in control of one's own destiny are generally the prime motivators. I have actually had buyers reject a business because all they could do with it is make money.

Buyers do not really want to buy your business or mine. They really would like to start a business of their own rather than buy ours. However, people will and do buy businesses when they see the opportunity to make the business theirs. There are no perfect businesses just as there are no perfect people. Something will be wrong with every business.

A buyer's perception of risk diminishes dramatically when he recognizes that all the right things are wrong with a business and that the business needs him and he knows what has to be done to improve the business and make it his.

A business is a vehicle whose future depends upon its driver. Will a new driver set records or drive the business into the ground? Unless a new owner recognizes the opportunities your business represents he obviously will not be able to capitalize upon them. No one knows what they don't know therefore, if opportunity is not recognized, it will not be capitalized upon.

Round Ball Theory

No one person is equally talented in all directions. We are not round balls. Some of us are footballs while others are Frisbees. None of us can do everything well. We are excellent at doing some things and good at others. There are tasks we don't like or want to do and others which we don't have a clue about. Our businesses reflect us and our skills, interests and lifestyle desires.

Putting it all Together

We begin by first "profiling" your business. We want to identify those things you do well and that got you where you are today. More importantly, we need to understand and identify what you have not done or have not done well. These areas describe the opportunities your business represents.

What we find is that the reverse or negative of your profile represents the profile of the "Right Buyer" for your business. Visualize a bell curve with the top representing what you do well and the extremes those things you don't do or don't do well. When we reverse this profile we see that the buyer has the ability to maintain what you have created and additionally, has the skills, talents and resources you lack and your company needs.

How do you find the right buyer for your business?

The same way you find a stranger in a crowd, with a picture or description of the person you seek. There are two ways of finding the right buyer. Either parade candidates through your business or walk the parade route and choose the candidate(s) of your liking.

We offer the "walk the parade route approach." We find out all that needs to be known about a candidate before they even know you are for sale. When we call you with a prospect we will be able to answer any questions as to why we feel we have the right buyer. We also want you to authorize our disclosing your identity. You may decide against a candidate for any number of reasons.

For example:
The candidate may be someone from within your industry thereby raising concerns about maintaining confidentiality. In any event you (the business owner) maintain control over the process."

Motivations – Perceptions – Value

Remember when we asked twelve people to value a business and received thirteen answers? One of the answers was much higher than the others. The person providing that answer was the right buyer and not because of the high price.

He was the right buyer because he recognized the opportunity the business represented and therefore voluntarily offered the highest price. Remember no one pays more for anything than what they think it is worth. He saw all the right things were wrong and recognized the opportunity for him to improve the business and make the business his own.

Value increases proportionately as perception of risk decreases. Financial professionals will convert their perception of risk to a mathematical expression they call a "Capitalization Rate" or "Cap Rate." The cap rate goes down as one's perception of risk diminishes and value goes up accordingly.

We also mentioned lender's reluctance to financing Goodwill or the value of a business in excess of its asset value. Their reluctance diminishes as might yours when presented with a buyer possessing the skills, talents and resources to bring your business to the next level.

Does this make any sense to you? (Close)

Business Owner: Why yes it does (Agreement but no question regarding our compensation so we continue on)

As previously mentioned, the first step of the process is purely advisory in nature and begins with our profiling your business. We will want to meet again where walls won't have ears and when you have an open ended time frame. That is to say, we will not have to stop the process in order for you to catch a plane or something. The session usually lasts an hour or two but we want the ability to continue longer if required.

We will eventually want information you would expect us to require – financials etc. We will provide you with a list. Also a tour of your facility either after hours or as a customer, vendor or fishing buddy will be necessary. Essentially we will be performing a buyer's Due Diligence Review in order to report to you the view of your company from the outside in.

When we have all the information and data we require it usually takes us two to three weeks to complete our report. When the review is completed we will want to meet with you and your spouse and perhaps you will want to invite your accountant and attorney (or any other possible team member) to this meeting.

Our experience, after completing the business profile and buyer identification process and presenting the Marketplace Position and Summary of Values report, is that forty percent of business owners elect not to sell at this time and choose another option instead.

When business owners decide immediate sale is not appropriate the business need not be exposed to the marketplace. (Only the business owner can weigh the personal gain against the financial rewards of selling).

Depending upon circumstances, you may decide to:

- increase the value, then sell
- hire a manager, take on a partner
- do a merger or joint venture
- establish an employee stock ownership plan (ESOP)
- go public or do a private placement
- engage a work out specialist
- refinance the company
- pack up the business and move it to Florida
- simply liquidate the enterprise
  We inform. You decide.

This disciplined two step approach has been in use for years by Investment Bankers. In fact, were the value of your business to contain two or three extra zeros, your business would probably be a Public Company and investment bankers would be performing essentially this same exercise for your board of directors. In the Public company parlance this process is often described as Strategic Planning or Maximization of Shareholder's Value.

You: "Does this approach make sense to you?"

Business Owner: Yes it does. By the way, how do you get paid?

You: "I'm so glad you asked. We get paid in two steps. First, because our initial work is purely advisory in nature we receive a Retainer. Then, if the decision is to go to market, we receive a Success Fee upon sale of your company."

"When the decision is made that a sale is appropriate and timely, finding the right buyer is fairly straight forward. Because we know who or what we are looking for we know where to look and how to position your company as an exciting opportunity for him to capitalize upon."

You: "Should we get started?"

Business Owner: What is your retainer?

You: "In order to answer that question may I ask a few questions?"

Business Owner: Agreement

You now ask a series of questions designed to determine the complexity and scope of the assignment. Some sample questions: Is the company computerized or do you keep company records in a shoe box? Are interim statements available? Do you use the services of an account or CPA? Do you use a payroll service? Can you provide sales data by product or segment? How many people besides you must be interviewed in order to gain a complete overview of the company, its operations and competitive environment?

You now can quote either in dollars certain, "I believe in your case we can do the work for our minimum retainer of $XX,XXX." Or in a range, "We estimate the retainer to be between $XX,XXX and XX,XXX. An initial retainer of $X,XXX seems appropriate to begin the process."

Additional Ammunition to be Used as Appropriate

Your prospective client may ask additional or follow on questions. Some of the more common questions are reviewed below.

The Profiling Process – What is covered?
To develop a business profile one first looks at operation items such as:

- staffing
- hours of operation
- product or service segmentation
- margins by segment

- market served
- competitive environment
- customer base
- industry trends
- industry outlook
- new developments
- management style
- sales and marketing plans
- systems and controls (both managerial and financial)
- sources of supply

By examining operations in this way, a comprehensive understanding of how the business is being run can be discerned. A review of this kind will usually point out opportunities that can be built upon, areas where improvements or corrections are in order, or trends which will indicate attention is required either to eliminate a negative situation or capitalize upon what buyers may perceive as opportunities.

After gaining an understanding of your company's operations a review of current and historic financial information is in order. Company's tax returns or financial statements are not an operating manual. In fact, most are mystery novels. By first understanding operations and the industry, much of the mystery hidden in the financial statements dissipates.

What does your financial review cover?

Our financial review of the company will usually include:

- Comparative Income Statements and Balance Sheets for 3 to 5 years
- Recast or normalized Income Statements and Balance Sheets for 3 to 5 Years
- Review of key ratios:
    Operating ratios
    Leverage ratios
    Liquidity ratios
    Coverage ratios
- Comparison with the industry
- Gross margin analysis
- Expenses analysis (normalized)
- Staffing analysis
- Projection of future profits
- Weighting of historic and projected profits

Tell me more about how you determine the right buyer for my company.

After profiling you and your business we are in position to identify the profile of your ideal acquirer. The operational and financial analyses will have identified and quantified strengths and areas in need of improvement. The ideal candidate must possess the skills and resources necessary to capitalize upon the opportunities identified.

The ideal successor's profile will be the reverse, or negative, of the profile developed for the company.

For example:

Present Management	Successor
Needs sales/marketing	Strong sales/marketing
Strong systems/controls	Maintain system and controls
Strong product development	Appreciate product
Weak finance	Strong finance
Average manager	Above average manager
Worn out	Energetic

You can now identify your successor by the skills, interests and resources required for your company to flourish. Those candidates that fail to fit this profile have no reason to know you are considering sale.

Why is identifying the proper buyer important?

You can pick and choose your response(s) from the list below.

1. If the present value of your business is insufficient to meet your needs, you need not expose it to the marketplace. Appropriate steps can be taken to increase the value of the business before marketing efforts begin.

2. By knowing how different buyers approach valuing businesses, you can predict what they might be willing to pay for your firm.

3. The person who recognizes the greatest opportunity will be more likely to pay an optimum value (value is in the eye of the beholder).

4. The future of your company depends on the quality and vision of the person operating it (future value is dependent upon operator). A significant portion of your life has been invested in this business. If you are to pass the baton to someone else, you probably want to see the business succeed and prosper.

5. To obtain optimum value, you most probably will be asked to participate in the financing (third parties are reluctant to participate in financing the acquisition of small or family businesses without some component of seller financing).

6. You do not want to be *forced* back into the business should the new operator fail. You are selling in order to move on with your life.

7. Knowing who and what type of acquirer you are seeking eliminates much of the need to parade possible buyers through your business. Instead, you can walk the parade route and logically pick your successor (sell it but do not let anyone know it's for sale).

8. By understanding which type of buyer is likely to find your business most attractive affords you the ability to more accurately judge the business's value (ask twelve people and you will get as many answers).

"Your competitor does not charge a retainer"

That is correct. If I went about selling businesses as they do I wouldn't charge a retainer either.

"There are no shortcuts to
any place worth going."

Anon.

Chapter Seven

Types of Buyers and What They Will Pay

The range of value that various buyer types will attribute to a business is staggering. One may see a business as worthless while another is willing to pay millions! The wide range of values is in direct proportion to the amount of opportunity perceived by the buyer. To fully appreciate this thought we first have to differentiate between opportunity and potential.

Opportunity Vs Potential

Business owners we have served over the years have consistently stressed the potential their businesses represent. They were unaware of the damage inflicted on their business's value by emphasizing its potential. It's a natural and innocent mistake that virtually everyone makes.

Perhaps the use of the word "potential" causes a flashback to when we were in school and teachers would explain to our parents - "Johnny has the potential to do much better if only..."

Yes, if only Johnny had applied himself he would have done much better. If buyers apply themselves, more or better than you, then certainly they will achieve more success than you have experienced.

"The Value of a Business is Directly Proportionate to the Opportunity a Buyer Perceives"

The problem is that the buyer's response to all this always seems to be, "If I am going to do it why should I pay *you* for what I will do?" Buyers will purchase because of the potential. They just *will not pay you for it* (however, they will pay for opportunity).

Opportunity, on the other hand, is perceived as being different than potential. Opportunity is already created. It's there. You created the opportunity, and are willing to let the newcomer reap the advantages of your hard work. Any reasonable person must be compelled to compensate you for the opportunity you have created. It's only right. Prices based upon opportunity are superior to those based upon potential.

Semantics? No, it's the difference between your leaving with a nice bonus or giving your business to someone as a going away present. The buyer who sees the most opportunity pays the highest price.

Different Buyers
Pay Different Prices

Buyers can be categorized into four broad groups. It is very important to understand the differences between them, how they think and how to identify them.

The Strategic Acquirer

Strategic acquirers are the best. They traditionally pay very high prices, and virtually always pay cash! Typically you will find that they are either public companies or very large private corporations.

The decisions are generally restricted to board rooms and usually revolve around considerations such as economies of scale, new channels of distribution, proprietary product lines, new technology, market share or presence, etc.

Typically the decision makers are not buying with their own personal funds. Public company protocol is cash deals or cash and equivalents, (stock). Price Earning Ratios will range from 15 times earnings to OMG, (Oh my God!).

These are the transactions one reads about in the press and of which films, TV shows and dreams are made.

To be attractive to a Strategic Acquirer a firm should fit the following acquisition criteria:

- Sales in excess of $20 million
- Proprietary process or product
- Suitable levels of management in place
- Unique market presence or share
- Synergistic fit with acquirer's goals
- Management willing to stay

Most Strategic Acquirers have a Corporate Development Officer or department. Research will yield names, addresses and telephone numbers of persons you may contact. A public library or the library at your nearest business school is a wonderful resource for this information. Stock brokers can also assist with information through their research sections regarding proposed plans and activities of targeted firms.

Obtaining "acquisition criteria" will provide an overview of what each target company is looking for. It is very common for these acquirers to expect existing management to stay on for an extended period of time.

Generally one has to read between the lines because very often purchases can be far afield of the acquisition criteria guidelines. Strategic acquisitions produce the highest values because the perceived opportunity is the greatest in this environment.

Example of why:

Major Market Widget Corp., (MMW), is a public company with 20 million shares issued. They perceive that the acquisition of Niche Market Widgets, (NMW), will increase the perceived value of their stock by two dollars per share or forty million dollars! Therefore any price they pay under forty million will be a bargain.

NMW had sales of twenty million and recast profits (more on this later) of one million dollars, and after tax earnings of two hundred twenty thousand dollars. MMW pays eleven million dollars for NMW. WOW! That's 50 times earnings, or OMG!

Sophisticated or Corporate Acquirer

This is a new and expanding buyer segment. Many casual observers fail to recognize this group. Their numbers have increased dramatically since the late eighties. Three major factors have contributed to this increase:

Wall Street's LBO Mania Ends

We are all familiar with the once prevailing Wall Street mania of buying and dividing up companies for huge profits. Junk bonds, highly leveraged deals and stories of financial wizardry were constantly in the news during the late eighties and early nineties.

This rags to riches philosophy is over. No more junk bond mania. Many investors and corporations have recognized the solid opportunities in private sector companies for the first time. Many have lowered "acquisition criteria" size requirements considerably as a result.

Middle Management Layoffs and Recession

Thousands of very talented, high networth executives are being released from their jobs as Corporate America trims down. Many turn to self employment as prospects for future employment become slim. They always wanted their own business anyway. Why not now?

Some will buy on their own. Others will band together, pooling their talents and resources, and acquiring existing firms.

Interest Rates at Lowest Level in Decades

With prevailing yields on CDs and other investments at low levels, the more entrepreneurial are forming Investor Groups whose prime purpose is to acquire existing companies. Many have "on the shelf CEOs" with whom they will do a joint venture acquisition. The displaced executive may have the talent to operate a substantial firm but will not have enough money to buy a suitable firm on his own.

This group brings a schooled approach to the acquisition process. They are accustomed to Public Company PE ratios, and they expect to "pay a lot for the muffler."

The focus is on opportunity for growth and they will have criteria that is very similar to that of the Strategic Acquirer. Size of the target company is important but not as important as the opportunity.

Two types that fall into this group are Investment Groups and High Net Worth Individuals.

The Investment Group, Investment or Holding Company is typically an organization formed to acquire private companies. These groups take many forms. An acquisition criteria that typifies both groups is as follows:

Investment or Holding Company:
- Sales from 10 million to 100+ million
- Earnings of at least 1 million
- Expect to invest considerable cash or equity
- Cash deal or some form of future payments to seller
- Pay 3 to 10 times earnings

Smaller Groups and High Net Worth Individuals:
- Sales from 2 million to 20 million
- Expect 6 figure earnings
- Ability to leverage the buy
- Expect seller participation in the financing
- Pay 3 to 7 times earnings

Types of businesses sought by both groups:
- Manufacture or distribution
- Proprietary process or product
- Niche market or have a specific industry preference
- Prefer management remain or stay for significant transition period

Our data base contains hundreds of these groups from all over the country and more and more from other parts of the world. We receive at least one phone call or mailing from these groups every day of the week. This group is very aggressive. They are armed with telemarketing personnel, slick direct mail pieces and they network extensively to maintain a "deal stream".

Hundreds of businesses might be reviewed before one is selected. One to three buys per year appears to be usual from this activity.

With the focus on opportunity these buyers tend to pay very fine prices that will take future profits into account. However, in using their own funds, or their investors' funds, these buyers will not and/or cannot pay prices paid by Strategic Acquirers. PE ratios seem to range from a low of 2 to a high of 10 with 4 to 7 being more common.

Examples:

A popcorn company with sales of $3 million is acquired for $4 million in cash. A distributor with $25K in assets and a $50K operating loss is sold for $575K in cash.

Both of these companies were purchased by opportunity buyers. The first was a public company, the second a small investor group.

The pop corn company had established a loyal following, brand recognition and channels of distribution that would be synergistic with the public company's operations.

The distributor had established a quasi proprietary product and unique channels of distribution in several test markets. All the buyer had to do was to complete the loop and reap the benefits. The buyer had the resources the founder lacked. "All the right things were wrong."

Financial or Lifestyle Buyer

Financial and Lifestyle buyers are the most plentiful. They tend to focus solely on the present and past. They will attribute any improvement in profits to their own efforts and will not pay prices based upon projections.

They will consider a price fair if the transaction can meet three criteria:

1. This group considers it un-American to pay all cash. They expect terms or the ability to finance the buy.
2. They consider a modest return on their cash into the deal as not being unreasonable.
3. They have families to feed so minimum living wages are expected from the business upon purchase. A wage commensurate with their initial investment is usually considered fair.

This group is primarily interested in purchasing a job. They will not buy unless they can see a FIT and the *potential* for making the business better.

The first two groups are focused almost exclusively upon opportunity and will take projections into account while Financial Buyers focus on the here and now. Therefore, Financial Buyers will pay less than Strategic or Corporate Buyers. PE ratios generally range between 2 to 4 times "recast earnings".

Without proper preparation and positioning most small businesses will attract only Financial, (potential) buyers. This need not be the case. Every business can be developed and prepared so as to be attractive to opportunity buyers. The next chapter will provide an overview of the factors that determine the type of buyer a business might be able to attract.

Industry Buyer

Industry Buyers can be either the "best" or the "worst" buyers. Many times they are the buyers of last resort. *If you have to sell, usually only industry buyers will buy.*

They are the best buyers when they have a strategic reason(s) to buy and know that you know the reason(s). Otherwise watch out!

You would be an Industry Buyer if you were considering the purchase of another firm similar to your own. What would you pay for your own company? An honest answer is usually "I see what you mean."

Most industry buyers look only to selected assets to determine value. They do not want to pay for goodwill. What is goodwill anyway?

A firm's value is comprised of several factors:

- Value of company assets
- Prospects for future profitability and growth
- Rights and knowledge

To illustrate the difference between an Industry Buyer and others let's look at a purchase price allocation by the opportunity buyer when compared with the industry buyer for the same business.

	Opportunity Buyer	Industry Buyer
Value of Assets transferred	$500,000	$200,000
Covenant not to compete	150,000	0
Consulting agreement	150,000	0
Goodwill	50,000	0
Total	$850,000	$200,000

The Industry buyer did not see any value in your willingness to train or consult (what could you teach him anyway?). He was not worried about you competing with him after the transfer (you were retiring to Florida anyway, weren't you?).

Your assets did not particularly impress him either. He has newer or better equipment. The fork lift would be a duplicate of what he already has. A particular product line would not be compatible with his operation so why don't you sell that separately?

Your customer list may have been of interest to him at one time. No need to pay for the customer list with you winding down as he probably assumes he will get them anyway.

Before one attempts to sell a business one should:

- Know the difference between the various buyer types
- Determine how to attract the best buyer
- Change a company's potential into opportunity

Only the Right Buyer
Pays the Right Price

We have highlighted that *"the person who sees the most opportunity will pay the highest price."* How do you figure this out? Consider a bell curve. The top represents the strengths of the business and its management. The two extremes reflect what management either hasn't been done or hasn't been done well.

The reverse or negative of this profile will represent the strengths of the optimum or best buyer. This buyer will see the weaknesses as opportunity. The perception of risk will be lower therefore the value higher. All the right things will be wrong! The buyer will recognize the opportunity to improve the business and make it their business. Buyers want to buy a business they can make their business.

The first step in determining what is the highest value of your client's company and who will pay it starts with the analysis and profiling of the business.

Summary of the
Marketplace of Buyers

What follows is a description of the four types of buyers active in today's marketplace. Their unique perspectives and motivations can and do result in a wide difference in the prices they individually are willing to pay. In one Case Study Example the values ranged from $165,000 to $1,250,000. Each used the same

Balance Sheet and Income Statement to calculate the value they were willing to pay.

On the next page we provide a summary description of each type of buyer and the price they would pay for a service business that included significant inventories. Company earnings were $215,000 and asset values were estimated at $165,000.

The Strategic Acquirer

- Typically a large firm, usually a Public Company
- Accustomed to long term planning
- Economic considerations are evaluated however, reason for acquisition is not always purely economic
- Acquisition prompted by such factors as:
  Establishing new markets
  Access to proprietary processes/products
  Acquire new technology
  New products for existing channels of distribution and vice versa

Price - $1,250,000
Basis of Valuation – Rationale is generally reserved to the board room

Strategic Acquirers Minimum Revenue requirements = $20,000,000+ unless the Company has unique and proprietary processes, technologies or products to add synergy, or provide the ability to enter markets

The Corporate or Sophisticated Acquirer
- Typically comes from a large company background
- Employs "schooled" approach when determining value
- Usually a high net worth individual, a group of individuals, an investor group, or a small corporation
- Focuses on current and future, rather than past
- Places primary emphasis on capitalization of earnings, and on the ability to finance and leverage a purchase

Price - $750,000
Basis of Valuation – Current Earnings and Estimate of Future Earnings

Corporate or Sophisticated buyers are often the buyer of choice as they regularly take future earnings into account when assessing value. However, to attract this buyer, prospects for future growth and profitability must be documented with credible and supportable assumptions.

The Financial or Lifestyle Buyer
- Usually an individual
- Significant training and assistance required as part of the purchase price
- Primary focus on income replacement and the opportunity to build equity
- Major emphasis placed on historic and current conditions
- Projections of future profits not considered
- Perception of risk is generally higher than strategic or corporate acquirers
- Perception of risk has a limiting effect on initial capital investments
- Usually requests significant levels of seller financing.

Price - $425,000
Basis of Valuation - Current Earnings

This buyer usually needs significant training and assistance from existing management as part of the purchase price. Additionally, this buyer's perception of risk would have a limiting effect on initial capital investments and heighten requests for significant levels of seller financing.

The Industry or Asset Buyer
An Industry buyer is often confused with a Strategic acquirer. Industry buyers lack strategic or synergistic motivations for purchasing a company. Unlike Strategic Acquirers, Industry buyers generally focus only upon selected assets and resist acknowledging a company's intangible value or "Goodwill."
- Usually from within the same, or affiliated, field as the company
- Primary focus is on a business' fixed assets
- Presumes that they will bring virtually all other value to the enterprise

Price - $165,000
Basis of Valuation – Asset Value

In most situations this buyer is buyer of last resort.
Exception to this rule occurs when:
1. Company earnings are not commensurate with invested capital or,
2. Operational skills are not readily transferable and firm lacks infrastructure for continuation with out present owner.

Different Businesses
Command Different Prices

It is important for you to understand the factors that drive a company's value.

Financial results are surprisingly not the most important factor driving a company's value. It is ultimately the buyer that determines value. Therefore it follows that identifying the person or firm willing to pay the highest price is most important. The value of a company lies in a buyer's view of its future. Financial results reflect only the past.

To identify the best buyer or customer for any business, you must first understand both objective and subjective elements within the company you represent. How does the firm appear from the outside in? To whom will problems appear as valuable and exciting opportunities?

Factors that drive a company's value:

- **Customer or Buyer Identification** should be the first item on a list of important factors that drive a company's value. Unfortunately, this factor usually does not receive the attention required. This is understandable since few of us are able to objectively view ourselves, our business or anything else we are very close to and emotionally involved with. Also, business owners and most advisors, although immersed in the business climate, are not familiar with driving marketplace forces or the various types and categories of buyers operating therein.

- **Opportunity** is an obvious factor that must be on everyone's list. But what is opportunity? Opportunity is different from potential. Buyers will pay for opportunity but not for potential. Why? Opportunity is perceived as having been created by the business owner and potential is that which will be created by the acquirer. Buyers will not pay you for what they will do (potential). They will pay for what you have done (opportunity). Perception of opportunity will vary depending on the type of buyer viewing it, emphasizing the critical need to know your customer.

- **Earnings** register high on most observers list of important factors. Since most private company's financial statements are driven by the owner's desire to minimize taxes, reported earnings are usually misleading. The numbers alone, even after recasting or normalizing, will not adequately reflect a firm's true value. The value of a company lies in a buyer's view of its future.

Businesses can be divided into four size and type groupings. Transaction structure and financial requirements will vary depending upon the size and type of company involved and Definition of Earnings, usual Price/Earnings ratios and Terms of Sale vary by classification as the table below illustrates.

Business Acquisition Protocols and Language Change

Acquisition Protocols and language change with the business culture and size.

Wall Street
- Earnings   > $1 Million
- Earnings Definition   After Tax Earnings
- Price/Earnings Ratio   10x to OMG*
- Usual Terms   Cash or equivalents
- Business Structure Well formed corporate structure
  * Oh my GOD!

Middle Market
- Earnings   > $500K to Low Millions
- Earnings Definition   Adjusted EBIT or EBITDA
  Sometimes EBIT or EBITD
- Price/Earnings Ratio   3x to 15x
- Usual Terms   Equity of 1 to 2x Earnings
  Bank & Owner Financing to all
  Cash
- Business Structure   Corporate structure developing

Upper Main Street
- Earnings   > $100K to $500K + or -
- Earnings Definition   Adjusted EBIT or EBITDA
- Price/Earnings Ratio   3x to 7x
- Usual Terms   Equity of 1 to 2x Earnings
  Limited Bank plus Owner Financing
- Business Structure   Limited corporate structure

Main Street
- Earnings $100K + or –
- Earnings Definition   EBITDA + Owner's Compensation
- Price/Earnings Ratio   2x to 4x
- Usual Terms   Equity of 80 to 120% of Earnings plus
  Owner Financing
- Business Structure   Very dependent upon owner
  Owner treats the business as a job

We will put these principles to work in the next chapter.

The early bird may get the worm, but the second mouse gets the cheese.

Unknown

Chapter Eight

How to Identify and
Find the "Right Buyer"

Attracting business opportunity buyers is a relatively easy task. All you have to do is spend money on advertising and wait for the telephone to start ringing. Finding motivated and realistic buyers is another story. Our ability to identify the buyer that is right for our client's company is why we are paid the "big bucks. "

More Operating Stats

60 to 1

In our first years of business brokerage my records show that it took twenty buyer interviews to get one offer and it took three offers to close one sale. Sixty buyer interviews resulted in one sale! No wonder we, as most business brokers, were spending at least eighty percent of our time working with buyers. Our sellers were getting the short end of the stick and they were paying us. Plus, we were working too hard for the money we were making.

Our interview process did evolve so that we no longer toured buyers on their first visit nor did we drag out the listing book for a buyer's perusal. We had added a sort of primer on How to Buy a Business to the first meeting instead. Our effectiveness in turning prospects into buyers improved significantly.

3 to 1

Our effectiveness would improve even more once we began "Profiling" buyers as well as businesses. Eventually my top producers would interview three buyers for every sale or one sale for every three buyers interviewed. We became up to twenty times more effective because of our conscious effort to give more service to fewer people. No more running around as a headless chicken. Focus instead.

Interviewing Presidents

We understood Business Opportunity Buyers didn't know what they want to buy and realized we needed a tool(s) to help them recognize the right business for them when they saw it. We also realized we had to show them how to buy it after they found it, if a sale was to take place.

We thought that perhaps our real job represented that of a Head Hunter or Career Counselor rather than a Real Estate Broker. We were, after all, interviewing future presidents and CEOs for our business owner clients. What tools did career counselors employ in assisting outsourced executives?

I contacted an acquaintance who was a career counselor and explained what I did and asked for direction. He agreed that we both were doing essentially the same job i.e. placing people in new careers. The first step he took, he explained, was to inventory the candidate's skills, resources, training and interests. Next was to suggest careers matching the skill sets of the candidate.

Once a career was chosen he would assist the candidate in:
a) contacting target employers b) writing the resume and preparing the candidate for the interview with the employer. In other words, help candidates find the right job and show them how to get it. Sounded familiar to us.

Buyer Profile and
Business Identification Workbook

We developed a tool, with the career counselor's aid, to assist us in helping our buyers find the business that would be right for them. We named the tool our "Buyer Profile and Business Identification Workbook." Buyers visiting us for the first time would now leave our offices with homework.

Career counselors use workbooks designed to reveal personality types and personal preferences. They suggest occupations or careers for the client's consideration based upon the workbook data. We would be doing essentially the same thing. We would suggest businesses that had an opening for a new president with their skills and talents (they could buy).

If we didn't have anything that fit them we would either:
1) Place them in our data base of buyers to be contacted when an appropriate opportunity came along or
2) Represent them in a pro-active search.

(We conducted searches on retainer plus success fee. The retainer ranged from $2,500 to $7,500 a month and the success fee was our usual percentage of sale price).

We usually were able to make at least one match although we preferred three. In fact we expected the first business we exposed the prospect to would be the one they would purchase and we told them so. We suggested they bring a check when we toured the business so they could make an offer and take the business off the market. We will have more on techniques later. But let's take a look at the workbook first.

"You are never given a wish without also being given the power to make it come true. You may have to work for it, however."

Richard Bach
___

Catch a man a fish, and you can sell it to him. Teach a
man to fish, and you ruin a wonderful business
opportunity.

Karl Marx

Buyer Profile
and
Business Identification
Workbook

Your Firm
Address
City, State Zip
Telephone
Email
Web site

Introduction

The ability to identify the type of business that best suits you is by far the single most important factor in determining your success in a business of your own. Ideally your business should match your interests, skills, aptitudes, resources and interests.

This workbook is designed to help you and us define the type of business that will be best for you. It may also support ideas you now have or perhaps suggest other possibilities.

Most people find filling out this workbook helpful and fun. Take your time. Don't rush. You will gain more by approaching this foundational task thoroughly. Use a pencil so you can make corrections easily.

Your Name _____

Address _____

City _____ State _____ Zip Code _____

Home Phone _____ Business Phone _____

E Mail _____ Facsimile _____

Cell Phone _____ Web Site www. _____

Date _____

Business Daydreams

List below the businesses you have considered when thinking about your future. List the businesses you have daydreamed about or have discussed with others.

Businesses

1	
2	
3	
4	
5	
6	
7	
8	

Areas of Special Interest

This section is devoted to those areas of interest that are significant to you: in particular, hobbies, sports, leisure activities, travel, gardening etc. Indicate your special interests below or use a separate sheet.

Special Interests:

Civic or Community Activities:

Association and Club Memberships:

Activities

Check off "Like" for those activities you enjoy doing. Check off "Dislike" for those things you dislike doing or are indifferent to.

M

	Like	Dislike
1. Repair cars		
2. Fix electrical items		
3. Build things with wood		
4. Drive trucks or tractors		
5. Take a woodworking course		
6. Take an auto repair course		
7. Work on a motorcycle or snowmobile		
8. Use metalworking tools		
9. Wallpaper a room		
10. Take a course in home design		

Total number of likes _____

I

	Like	Dislike
1. Read scientific books or magazines		
2. Write computer programs		
3. Build model rockets		
4. Work in a laboratory		
5. Solve math or chess puzzles		
6. Take a biology course		
7. Take a chemistry course		
8. Study geology		
9. Take a physics course		
10. Take a computer programming course		

Total number of likes _____

A

	Like	Dislike
1. Draw, paint or sketch		
2. Attend plays		
3. Design furniture or buildings		
4. Play in a band or orchestra		
5. Attend recitals, concerts or musicals		
6. Take art classes		
7. Read or write poetry		
8. Read popular fiction		
9. Create portraits or photographs		
10. Design a garden or landscape		

Total number of likes _____

Activities continued

S

	Like	Dislike
1. Write letters or email to friends		
2. Attend religious services		
3. Belong to social clubs		
4. Help others with personal problems		
5. Take care of children		
6. Go to parties		
7. Dance		
8. Attend sporting events		
9. Attend meetings and conferences		
10. Meet new people		

Total number of likes _____

E

	Like	Dislike
1. Influence others		
2. Sell something		
3. Discuss politics		
4. Operate own business or service		
5. Attend conferences		
6. Give talks		
7. Serve as officer of any group		
8. Supervise the work of others		
9. Meet important or influential people		
10. Lead a group in accomplishing a goal		

Total number of likes _____

C

	Like	Dislike
1. Keep your room and desk clean		
2. Type papers for yourself or others		
3. Manipulate numbers in bookkeeping or business		
4. Work at a computer		
5. Keep detailed records of expenses		
6. Take a business course		
7. Take a bookkeeping course		
8. File reports, letters, etc.		
9. Write business letters		
10. Take a computer course		

Total number of likes _____

Occupations

Indicate the occupations that interest you by checking "Yes" for those you like and "No" for those you dislike or find uninteresting.

M

	Yes	No
1. Airplane mechanic		
2. Auto mechanic		
3. Carpenter		
4. Power equipment operator		
5. Surveyor		
6. Tree surgeon		
7. Long distance truck driver		
8. Electrician		
9. Plumber		
10. Machinist		

Total number of Yes _____

I

	Yes	No
1. Meteorologist		
2. Biologist		
3. Medical lab technician		
4. Anthropologist		
5. Zoologist		
6. Geologist		
7. Write scientific articles		
8. Dentist		
9. Botanist		
10. Researcher		

Total number of Yes _____

S

	Yes	No
1. Sociologist		
2. High school teacher		
3. Juvenile delinquent expert		
4. Marriage counselor		
5. Speech therapist		
6. School principal		
7. Clinical psychologist		
8. Vocational counselor		
9. Personnel director		
10. Youth program director		

Total number of Yes _____

Occupations continued

E

	Yes	No
1. Sales manager		
2. Sports promoter		
3. Publicity director		
4. Real estate broker		
5. Master of ceremonies		
6. Salesperson		
7. Restaurant manager		
8. Business executive		
9. Manufacturer's representative		
10. Advertising executive		

Total number of Yes _____

A

	Yes	No
1. Poet		
2. Musician		
3. Author		
4. Artist		
5. Free lance writer		
6. Journalist		
7. Singer		
8. Composer		
9. Cartoonist		
10. Playwright		

Total number of Yes _____

C

	Yes	No
1. Bookkeeper		
2. Business teacher		
3. Budget reviewer		
4. CPA		
5. Bank teller		
6. Tax attorney		
7. Financial analyst		
8. Bank examiner		
9. Comptroller		
10. Computer operator		

Total number of Yes _____

Competencies

Indicate the activities that you can do well by checking "Yes." Check "No" for those activities you perform poorly or have never performed.

M

	Yes	No
1. I have used wood shop power tools		
2. I can adjust a carburetor		
3. I can operate a grinder or sewing machine		
4. I can read blueprints		
5. I can repair furniture		
6. I can make plumbing repairs		
7. I can make simple electrical repairs		
8. I can refinish furniture		
9. I can make mechanical drawings		
10. I can hang wallpaper		

Total number of Yes _____

I

	Yes	No
1. I can name 3 foods high in protein		
2. I understand the "half life" of a radioactive element		
3. I can use a microscope		
4. I can identify 3 constellation of stars		
5. I can describe the function of white blood cells		
6. I can interpret a simple chemical formula		
7. I understand why satellites do not fall to earth		
8. I have participated in a science fair or contest		
9. I can create simple computer programs		
10. I can calculate the "present value" of future payments		

Total number of Yes _____

S

	Yes	No
1. I can play a musical instrument		
2. I can participate in multi-part choral singing		
3. I can perform as a musical soloist		
4. I can act in a play		
5. I can do interpretive reading		
6. I can sketch people so that they can be recognized		
7. I can paint or sculpt		
8. I can make pottery		
9. I write stories or poetry well		
10. I can design clothing, posters or furniture		

Total number of Yes _____

Competencies continued

E

	Yes	No
1. I have been elected to an office		
2. I can supervise the work of others		
3. I have unusual energy and enthusiasm		
4. I am good at getting people to do things my way		
5. I am a good salesperson		
6. I won an award as a salesperson or leader		
7. I have organized a club, group or gang		
8. I have started my own business or service		
9. I am a good debater		
10. I know how to be a successful leader		

Total number of Yes _____

S

	Yes	No
1. I am good at explaining things to others		
2. I have participated in charity or benefit drives		
3. I cooperate and work well with others		
4. I can be a good host/hostess		
5. I can teach children easily		
6. I can plan entertainment for a party		
7. I am a good judge of personality		
8. I can plan a school or church social affair		
9. I am good at helping people who are upset or troubled		
10. I have done work as a volunteer		

Total number of Yes _____

C

	Yes	No
1. I can type 40 words a minute		
2. I can operate a computer		
3. I have held an office job		
4. I can use an accounting software program		
5. I can post credits and debits		
6. I can do a lot of paperwork in a short time		
7. I clear my work space at the end of each day		
8. I can keep accurate records of payments or sales		
9. I can prepare my own tax return		
10. I can prepare an Income Statement		

Total number of Yes _____

Self Estimates

		High			Average			Low
M	Mechanical Ability	7	6	5	4	3	2	1
	Manual Skills	7	6	5	4	3	2	1
	Total M _____							
I	Scientific Ability	7	6	5	4	3	2	1
	Math Ability	7	6	5	4	3	2	1
	Total I _____							
A	Artistic Ability	7	6	5	4	3	2	1
	Musical Ability	7	6	5	4	3	2	1
	Total A _____							
S	Teaching Ability	7	6	5	4	3	2	1
	Friendliness	7	6	5	4	3	2	1
	Total S _____							
E	Sales Ability	7	6	5	4	3	2	1
	Managerial Skills	7	6	5	4	3	2	1
	Total E _____							
C	Clerical Ability	7	6	5	4	3	2	1
	Office Skills	7	6	5	4	3	2	1
	Total C _____							

How to Organize Your Answers

Place the number of Like and Yes answers for each group in the appropriate position below.

Activities

    M   I   A   S   E   C

Occupations

    M   I   A   S   E   C

Competencies

    M   I   A   S   E   C

Self Estimates

    M   I   A   S   E   C

Total Scores

    M   I   A   S   E   C

Place the letters with the highest scores in the boxes below. If two scores are the same put both letters in the same box

SCORE

Highest	Second	Third

Specific Skills and Knowledge

We all have more skill, knowledge and comfort in some areas as compared to others. Listed below are specific areas where you can rate your level of skill and comfort on a scale of 1 – 10 with 10 being the highest level of your skill, knowledge or comfort. Circle your answer.

Level	Low				Medium				High	
Accounting	1	2	3	4	5	6	7	8	9	10
Finance	1	2	3	4	5	6	7	8	9	10
Taxes	1	2	3	4	5	6	7	8	9	10
Sales	1	2	3	4	5	6	7	8	9	10
Marketing	1	2	3	4	5	6	7	8	9	10
Sales Mgmt	1	2	3	4	5	6	7	8	9	10
Managerial	1	2	3	4	5	6	7	8	9	10
Motivational	1	2	3	4	5	6	7	8	9	10
Analytical	1	2	3	4	5	6	7	8	9	10
Verbal	1	2	3	4	5	6	7	8	9	10
Writing	1	2	3	4	5	6	7	8	9	10
Mechanical	1	2	3	4	5	6	7	8	9	10
Design	1	2	3	4	5	6	7	8	9	10
Computer	1	2	3	4	5	6	7	8	9	10
Programming	1	2	3	4	5	6	7	8	9	10
Systems	1	2	3	4	5	6	7	8	9	10
Controls	1	2	3	4	5	6	7	8	9	10
Concepts	1	2	3	4	5	6	7	8	9	10
Manual	1	2	3	4	5	6	7	8	9	10
Other	1	2	3	4	5	6	7	8	9	10

Lifestyle and Financial Requirements

The right business must fit your lifestyle and financial needs. Please complete the following section.

Time distance of business from your home _____ hour(s) _____ minutes

Are you willing to move for the right business? ____ Yes   No ___

Earliest start time desired _____ A.M. Latest acceptable stop time _____ P.M.

Minimum take home compensation (start) required $ _____ per month

Is family member's participation in the business important? Yes ___ No ___

Participation in the business to be: Full Time ___ Part Time ___ Absentee ___ Seasonal ___

Activity level desired: High ____ Medium ____ Low ____

Prefer work environment to be: Inside ___ Outside ___ Both ___ Doesn't matter ___

Travel: Prefer travel ___ Some travel OK ___ Prefer No Travel ____

Overnight Travel: OK ___ Sometimes ___ None ___

Should the business address hobbies? Yes ___ No ___

Customer contact: High ___ Medium ___ Low ___ None ___

Would you rather: Customers come to you ____ You go to them ____

Prefer customers to be: General public ___ Business people ____ Doesn't matter ____

Aversion to specific products/services (liquor, chemicals etc.) If yes please explain.

Other:

Financial Information

Preferred Price Range of Business from $ _____ to $ _____

Preferred Initial Investment   from $ _____ to $ _____

Total Available for Down Payment $ _____

Personal Draw Required (Annual) $ _____

<u>Source of Funds:</u>

Cash in banks $ _____

Equity in Real Estate $ _____

Marketable Securities $ _____

401K etc. $ _____

Family $ _____

Investors $ _____

Other _____ $ _____

Your net worth $ _____

Comments:

Educational Background

Please summarize below your educational background including special interest courses or include your résumé in place of this section.

Business Experience

Please summarize your work experience including any information that would be helpful in identifying your ideal business. You may substitute a résumé in place of this section.

The Same Story

We began to notice that we were using the same words to describe the buying process to buyers that we used when describing the selling process to sellers. That fact was driven home one day when, after an initial buyer interview, the "buyer" revealed he was actually a business owner pretending to be a business buyer. He wanted to understand the process different brokers used before he hired one to represent his business.

I explained our process of selling businesses was essentially the same process I just outlined, with a few minor modifications, when I thought he was a buyer.

He remarked that "Your methods are certainly different from those of the others I have interviewed. I am impressed that you didn't have to change your tune as the others did. Truths need not be changed." He hired us on the spot and we picked up our $5,000 retainer the next day. We sold his business several months later. The success fee was $35,000.00.

What's the Story?

You will recall how our interview with a possible sell side client began. First, be sure to make your visitor feel welcome. Offer coffee, soft drink or water as you would a guest in your home. Next ask what he is seeking. How many businesses has he looked at and so forth until it is appropriate for you to hold court.

The components of a buyer interview were essentially the same as the sell side presentations.
- Brief introduction of yourself and your firm
- Overview of why buying a business is different from buying essentially anything else
- The essential facts to be woven into a buy side presentation include:
  - Buyers usually don't know exactly what type of business they want to buy. However, as with art they will know the right business when they see it.
  - Buyers really would rather start a business of their own rather than buy one
  - Motivation to buy or sell a business is seldom money
  - Buyers really want - "All the right things to be wrong."
  - No one is equally talented in all directions (no one is a "Round Ball")
  - Future success of the business depends on new owner's skills

- Banks reluctant to lend on goodwill (goodwill being the business' value in excess of its asset value)
- Neither Buyer, Seller or their advisors know what a business is worth but all have an opinion
- No one pays more for anything than they believe it is worth

The First Interview

After illustrating the unique environment in which businesses are bought and sold we explain how we "profile" each of our client companies and how that profiling reveals the strengths and resources required of the new presidents we seek. Those strengths should match the areas of opportunity the company represents.

The profiling approach is important to everyone involved in the business and with the transaction because:
- Confidentiality is maintained by limiting exposure of the company in the marketplace, a breach of which could severely damage or destroy the business. Typically we need to expose a client company to three or less possible acquirers. Most often it is the first buyer exposed to the company that buys it.
- Business gets the new leadership it requires to take it to the next level.
- Buyer obtains an exciting opportunity to improve the business and make it his own.
- Seller more likely to participate in financing the transaction because of heightened confidence in the buyer's abilities to repay the note.
- Banks and other lenders also more likely to participate in financing a transaction for the same reason.
- Employee's career opportunities and job security enhanced
- Customers continue to be well served.

Give if You Want to Get

We believe that in order to get one has to give first. Therefore rather than simply asking "How much money do you have and where is it?" we would give the candidate an overview of what differing levels and types of business might cost as summarized in the Business Acquisition Protocol and Business Valuation Matrix Exhibit found on the following page.

Business Acquisition Protocol and
Business Valuation Matrix

Transaction structure and financial requirements will vary depending upon the size and type company involved. Businesses can be divided into four classes. Definition of Earnings, usual Price/Earnings ratios and Terms of Sale vary by classification.

Wall Street
Usually public or very large private companies

Earnings:	Measured in Millions
Earnings Definition:	After Tax Earnings
Price/Earnings Ratio:	10x to OMG*
Usual Terms:	Cash or equivalents

* Oh my GOD!

Middle Market
Generally private companies with well defined corporate structure

Earnings:	$500K to Low Millions
Earnings Definition:	EBIT , EBIT-D, EBIT-DA to After Tax Earnings
Price/Earnings Ratio:	3x to 15x
Usual Terms:	
Down Payment:	Equity of 1 to 2x earnings to all Cash
Plus:	Bank note(s) and owner financing

Companies that represent a "Strategic Fit" usually will be valued and sold using "Wall Street" protocol. When a strategic reason for purchase is lacking, "Upper Main Street" methods are generally employed.

Upper Main Street
Private companies with corporate structure developing where owner has delegated many functions to others

Earnings:	Usually under $500K
Earnings Definition:	Adjusted EBIT or EBIT-DA, Sometimes EBIT and EBIT-D are used
Price/Earnings Ratio:	3x to 7x
Usual Terms:	
Down Payment:	Equity of 1 to 2x earnings
Plus:	Owner financing - limited bank involvement

Main Street
Commonly referred to as "Mom and Pop" businesses where owner wears "all the hats."

Earnings:	Usually under $100K
Earnings Definition:	Discretionary Earnings
Price/Earnings Ratio:	1x to 4x
Usual Terms:	
Down Payment:	80% to 120% of earnings
Plus:	Owner financing - Bank financing is rare

Definition of Terms:
EBIT = Earnings Before Interest and Taxes
EBITD = Above plus Depreciation
EBIT-DA = Above plus non-recurring and discretionary expenses
Discretionary Earnings = EBIT-DA plus Owner's Compensation
Note: Down payments or equity investments may exceed the levels indicated when inventories and other current asset values are high.

Give Out the Homework

We would point out that each of our client companies had paid us a retainer and were serious about selling. More to the point, our clients knew what skills, talents and resources they wanted the business buyer to posses.

We would then introduce our "Buyer Profile and Business Identification Workbook" and ask that they and their spouse, spousal substitute or partner complete the workbook and return it to us prior to our next meeting. We strongly suggested both parties attend the next meeting to obtain the best results.

At the next meeting we would review the workbook they had returned to us. The meeting's objective was basically to confirm that we had interpreted their answers correctly.

The Second Interview

Review the Workbooks

We reviewed the workbook prior to the buyer's return to our office. Now we review the workbook with them. The workbook is a catalyst for our understanding the candidate's strengths and preferences. Remember we are using the workbook as a tool for the buyer to describe his skills, talents, preferences and wishes for and to us. We need confirmation that we have the profile and preferences correctly identified. They tell us. We do not tell them.

Once we agree on the buyer's "Profile," we outline the acquisition process and begin Buyer Education in earnest. The workbook has provided insight as to our buyer's level of comfort and proficiencies in many areas. It also provides strong clues as to the level and type of education our candidate will require from us.

Give Information BEFORE it is Needed

Our job now is to provide information the buyer will need before it is needed. If you attempt to provide the same information during the heat of negotiations your efforts will probably be resisted as typical salesman's tactics. The same data provided before it is needed is usually welcomed and received as sincere, helpful and informative. Some of the most common areas requiring educational attention are:
- Use of professional advisors
- Pricing

- Interpreting financial statements
- Determining their probable gross profit results

Use of Professional Advisors

A library of books can be written on the subject of correctly using professional advisors. However, in the interest of brevity, here is a story my wife told me. She had listened to my complaints regarding "run-away" attorneys and accountants killing deals for years and had just finished reading something she thought addressed the issue head on.

A young couple approaches their clergyman and ask "Should we get married?" The clergyman's answer is a resounding NO! "Why?" the couple asks? The clergyman answeres, "If you have to ask me that question you obviously don't know what you are doing."

Here's how I relate this story to buying a business. Imagine a fellow who, considering the purchase of a business, approaches his life long accountant friend armed with five years of tax returns. He then askes the question, "Should I buy this business?" or "How much money will I make if I buy this business?"

Now I ask you to put yourself in the shoes of your pal the accountant. Has'nt the question "Should I buy this business" sent a chill up your spine? Asking that question alone strongly suggests that your entrepreneurial friend doesn't know what he is doing. Are you going to let him hurt himself by buying the business?

Imagine the answer were you to ask an attorney the same thing. Is there any question what the answer might be given today's litigious environment? It is against most all professional's codes of ethics to recommend clients follow destructive or dangerous courses of action regardless of legal liabilities incurred by such actions.

Array of Advisors

We all have many advisors in our lives that we call upon for different reasons. These advisors include attorneys, accountants, clergy, mechanics, stock brokers and others. To obtain the best results we must understand our role and responsibilities when seeking advice and/or services from our professionals.

The best way to use your professional(s) is to first realize that the decisions are yours to make and not theirs. In the case of buying a business, you do the research and analysis. When you are finished and believe you fully understand the opportunity, you present your findings to your accountant and ask, "Have I done it correctly and have I missed anything?" If you are this entrepreneur's long time friend aren't you more comfortable than you would be if instead he asked "Should I buy this business?" or "How much can I make if I buy this business?"

The scope of your attorney's assignment should be limited to setting up your corporation (if requested), document review for fairness and language interpretation and implications of various options. The attorney answers and you decide. Remember the "He, We, I syndrome" mentioned earlier.

No Price on the Menu

We do not place a price on any of the businesses we represent. It doesn't matter whether it's a Main Street or Middle Market business. We do not provide a price for our buyers. There are several good reasons for this.

Corporate buyers do not necessarily expect a price but essentially all individuals and small company acquirers do. We all expect a price posted on items offered for sale. Real estate listings include a price so why not our business offerings?

Reason - One can finance the entire purchase of just about anything imaginable except the purchase of small businesses. The sale of a small business usually will involve some component of seller financing and that changes the pricing dynamics dramatically.

Obviously seller financing means the seller does not receive the entire purchase price upon sale. How much will be paid at closing? How long will it take before the seller is paid in full? Does the seller have confidence in the buyer's abilities to run the business successfully?

Behold the turtle, he makes progress only when he
sticks his neck out.

Bruce Levin

Price Isn't Important!

It's not what you pay, it's how you pay it combined with who you are that determines a price that is acceptable to a seller.

Wise Guy Example

I often use a wise guy example to illustrate why price is not important. First let's acknowledge that no one will pay more for anything than they believe it is worth even if it is you or I doing the selling.

I will allege that the owner refused an offer of five million dollars for the business (a business expected to be priced at a small fraction of that number)! The owner liked the price but not the terms. The offer was one dollar a week to be paid for five million weeks. This is an excellent example of the old adage "I'll pay your price if you will accept my terms" in action.

I was given a wise guy answer by a candidate who thought a seller might accept such an offer if we could guarantee the seller would be around to collect the last payment. Although the candidate's thinking addresses the reality that one's motivation to sell is not usually the money alone, the terms are still a bit extreme. But, who knows?

Provides a safety feature for the buyer

We will ask the buyer. Do you know what you don't know? Will you know when you don't recognize the full opportunity a business represents? Our businesses are priced fairly and reasonable terms will be accepted. Those recognizing the opportunities our offering represents will offer the right price.

If you do not offer an acceptable price it is probably because you do not see the value of the opportunity. One cannot capitalize upon unrecognized opportunity.

The good news is that in this process it is difficult to buy a business when the business's full opportunity is not recognized.

How to Determine Real Earnings

The Buyer Profile and Business Identification workbook may have indicated a lack of financial savvy on the part of our candidate. In any event our candidate must understand that the real earnings of any small business will not be found on the "bottom line." The candidate must know how to read between the lines when determining real profits, and we have to make sure they know how to do it. Otherwise the buyer will be asking the accountant "How much can I make if I buy this business."

Determining the real income of small and mid-size businesses, especially cash businesses, can be a challenge. It is our job to make sure our candidates understand how to do it. Here is an outline of how the subject might be addressed.

You need only three numbers to determine the profitability of any business:
1. Revenues or sales
2. Necessary expenses
3. Cost of goods

Maximums and Minimums

Revenues shown on tax returns can usually be considered minimums and the expenses maximums. An occasional dime may fall through the cracks and not be recorded. However, seldom are expenses overlooked or forgotten when preparing tax returns. It is these two numbers that are being purchased and typically do not change with management. Customers will continue to trade with the business. Rent, utilities and other expenses will remain essentially the same the day after a business transfers ownership as the day before.

Cost of Goods

Cost of Goods or Sales is truly dependent upon management's abilities. You should rely on your own independent assessment of what these costs will likely be under your management. You are not buying management, you are replacing it.

Cost of Goods or Sales represents the cost of products, goods or services sold by the company. In manufacturing environments this number is referred to as Cost of Sales and includes cost of labor involved in production of the products. In most other situations such as restaurants, retail and service businesses, Cost of Goods represents the cost of goods purchased for resale. Labor is usually included under expenses.

Gross Profit Test

In order to obtain an understanding of what the cost of goods might be under your management it is recommended that you conduct a gross profit test. To perform such a test you simply record the price of products being sold and then determine the cost of same to the business. From this data gross profit by product can be determined and gross profit for the firm can be estimated. Your findings can then be measured against industry data.

Because cost of goods/sales are low or high under present management's control does not mean the same will be true on your watch. How the product/service is priced is your business. By conducting a Gross Profit Test you gain an understanding of pricing dynamics plus a clearer view of operations.

Example

Revenues for this small specialty retailer are $1,000,000. The research and gross profit test you conducted indicate cost of sales under your management should approximate 35%. Necessary expenses (rent etc.) from the tax return are $300,000. The COG on the tax return may be higher or lower than your Gross Profit Test estimates. Before using your estimates you should be comfortable in your knowledge of why this is the case and your ability to perform differently.

The simple math

Revenues	$1,000,000	
Cost of Goods	350,000	35% (Under your mgmt)
Gross Profit	650,000	65%
Expenses	300,000	30%
Estimated Profit	$350,000	35%

Industry operational data sources

A trip to a good business library or surfing the net will reveal much valuable information including usual cost of goods/sales data for use in ratifying the reasonableness of your estimates.

Some of the better sources of operational data include:
- Robert Morris Associates
- Dun & Bradstreet - Comparative Statements Studies
- Financial Research Associates - Financial Studies of the Small Business

What do those letters mean?

You can probably guess the meanings from the questions being asked under each letter. If not we offer the following:

M = Mechanical – Important for a business which relies on equipment or machinery for the production of revenues.

I = Investigative – MBAs and CPAs usually score high in this category.

A = Artistic – Important when dealing with subjective businesses such as florist and interior decorating businesses.

S = Scientific – Can be important when dealing with objective businesses such as machining companies or engineering firms.

E = Enterprising – The candidate should score the highest here. If not you may not have a real buyer.

C = Conventional – Task oriented businesses such as retail stores would generally appeal to this person

Example of an interpretation:

E M A - This person would be entrepreneurial (a must), mechanically inclined and posses an artistic eye. We might introduce this buyer to a printing company assuming other factors are a match. The machinery involved would not necessarily be intimidating and an artistic eye is beneficial to anyone in the graphic arts business (printing).

How do you Attract Buyers?

Buyers can be attracted to this process in all the usual ways i.e. classified ads, internet postings and trade publications but the best buyers come from referrals from others in the "Deal Stream." Remember our "Take an Advisor to Lunch" program referenced earlier. Those contacts proved to be the source of our best buyers.

These buyers were the ones with the "White Heat Passion" to acquire a business. Typically they had been to every business broker in the area, looked at scores of businesses, usually had made at least one offer that failed to pan out and now were networking with CPAs, bankers, lawyers etc. in search of their business.

It was this group of buyers who immediately embraced our process with enthusiasm. If we had a match for them a sale was soon to follow. If we didn't have something for them a large percentage would engage us to find them a business. It was for this group that we initially developed our Buyer Representation Program.

"There's no business like show business, but there are several businesses like accounting"

David Letterman

Chapter Nine

Developing the Report

Your objectives in the first interview with your new client are: gain an understanding of company operations and environment, obtain your retainer and agreement. If the meeting is held at your offices then a tour of the business and the gathering of tax returns and other documents will follow at another date.

We want to fully understand the business and the opportunity it represents in order to determine the optimum price and best buyer. We are basically performing a "Due Diligence Review." We must see everything a buyer and their advisors will want to see. Our expertise lies in knowing and understanding the marketplace and the buyers within it. We know how they think, what turns them on or off. We understand how different types of buyers determine business value. Our report will reflect perceptions and reactions of buyers and their advisors as to the opportunity the company represents to them.

My Left-hand Man

Salespeople are notorious for being poor at doing paperwork and CPAs, MBAs, PhDs and other financial professionals are often equally poor as salespeople. This observation has been confirmed by doctors and others studying brain activity. They have divided brain activities into two general groups and assigned a hemisphere of the brain to each.

Selling tends to be a right brain activity while detailed activities such as accounting usually are considered left brain activities. Others refer to personality distinctions as Hunter and Farmer thought processes. The hunter must be willing to change direction and objective as situations dictate even if it means being away from home for an extended period. Conversely, the farmer must be content to stay put and consistently tend to the farm.

Curiosity as to what's on the other side of the mountain looses to a need to milk the cows both in the morning and again in the evening.

We would point out to the client that because we ourselves are not Round Balls we employ a team approach to important assignments. Each team has a "Right Brain" and a "Left Brain" member to help insure a quality work product. Clients really appreciated our team approach to Profiling their business.

I would explain that just as they could not be all things for their business neither could I. Because I was more sales orientated (right brain) I would rely on my "Left-hand Man" (or woman) to assist with the creation of our report. This left-hand man business may sound fairly silly but it made sense to our clients and helped to increase our efficiency in selling businesses.

The Mechanics:

Gathering information

We developed data gathering sheets to assist us in the interview process. The sheets are neccessary to make sure we don't leave anything out. Generally, one answer leads to a different question and as a result interviews tend to be rather free flowing. The Profile topics are not intended or expected to be all inclusive. Additional topics and areas of interest will arise in essentially every interview. Listed below is an overview of the major areas of discussion.

The Company
The Company - number of stockholders, its form.

History
The company's beginnings - how it got to where it is now.

The Industry
Industry outlook - obtain information on trade associations and publications in order to ratify opportunities using third party sources.

Market Served
Who are the customers, what is the outlook for their business. What other markets might the company serve?

Marketing Area
Outlook for the region served, demographics etc.

Customer Concentrations
What customer dependency exists if any? Breakdown of sales by customer.

Sales Segmentation
Revenues by product or business segment including target margin information. Be sure to gain an understanding of how your client prices services and products.

Operations
Hours and days open – seasonality

Staff
Ask for a list of employees by position, function. Include tenure, number of hours worked, wage/salary, date of last raise Identify family members. Will they stay or leave?   If the client uses a payroll service you might ask for both last year's YE summary and the most current summary.

Financial
Obtain federal tax returns and/or accountant's statements for minimum of three years, interim statements, sales by month for at least 3 years.

Facilities
Obtain copy of facility and any equipment leases.

Equipment
List of all equipment including, age, owner's considered opinion of Fair Market Value, (appraisal is best) condition and suitability. Suggest you have owner sign and date the list.

Competition
Obtain an overview of the competitive environment.

Environmental
Are there environmental issues or concerns?

Governmental
Are there rules or regulations pending that impact or may impact this business or industry?

The Opportunity
Gain a comprehensive understanding of the opportunity the business represents. In what areas can the acquirer make a positive difference?

Analysis

Thank goodness for computer programs. Analyzing financial results, whether it's comparing a company's results with those of its industry or computing scores of ratio calculations, can be quite tedious. It is especially so for the "Right Brains" among us. The software accompanying this writing eliminates most of the tedium usually associated with financial analysis.

Financial

We will analyze the company's past and present financial statements and prepare projections as may be required to predict future results including: recasting, ratio analysis, and analysis of all financial and operating information.

This entails developing comparative Income Statements and Balance Sheets for at least a three year period – five is better. From this data comparative ratio analyses can be developed to identify trends and comparisons with industry results.

After arranging historic financial results as above you will adjust both the Balance Sheet and Income Statement to adjust out tax code considerations. Balance sheet assets and liabilities are adjusted to reflect actual fair market values (FMV). Items not to be included in a possible sale are adjusted out.

The Income Statement or Profit and Loss should be normalized by adding back non cash expenses (excess depreciation), interest, and amortization, discretionary and non-recurring expenses. Expenses new owners will incur such as higher rent or labor expense to replace a presently non-paid bookkeeping spouse are deducted.

Industry comparison (when applicable)
Data used most often comes from Robert Morris and Associates, a financial reporting firm, but may emanate from other sources as well. Dun and Bradstreet and industry trade associations are the two most common sources in addition to Robert Morris.

The purpose of this exercise is to determine strengths and weaknesses of the company, and ratify the opportunity the company represents. For example: Assume Cost of Goods sold for the company is much higher than comparison with the industry would indicate. Does this indicate opportunity? Perhaps systems and controls need improvement or there is a hole in the cash register drawer that needs to be plugged.

Chapter Ten

Paperwork

As you transition to a fee based practice your contracts and forms should change as well as the words you use to describe yourself and your activities. The listing contract used for a Main Street Pizza shop is not necessarily appropriate for a twenty million dollar machine shop. As you position yourself as an advisor, standard forms should be replaced by letter formats. Listing Agreements are replaced by Letters of Authorization or Engagement.

Letter format agreements can be used for any size business whereas a "standard listing" form really cannot. You can transform your listing agreement into a letter format very easily with today's technology. Just make sure you change or eliminate any words that might confuse your client. You will notice no reference to BROKER, LISTING or FEE in any of the attached documents.

The documents provided here for your use have been extracted from our bizFORMS 4.0 software package. You may wish to eliminate or add language as you deem appropriate. For example, you might decide to eliminate the following language from your ENGAGEMENT letter when dealing with small companies. *"The Company agrees that upon consummation of the Transaction, Your Firm may, at its expense, announce to the business community through the Wall Street Journal and other appropriate media its role in effecting the transaction."*

You will notice a sliding scale Transaction Fee that breaks the first million in sale price into two parts. As example, you might use 12% of the first $500,000 and either 10% or 8% of the second $500,000 for a blended rate of 10% or 11% on the first million. The reason for this reflects the reality that:
- Most smaller businesses will have a sale price under a million dollars
- The costs to sell a small company are disproportionately high
- Reinforces the "We primarily sell large companies but we can sell your smaller business as well" position we prefer

Paperwork is not glamorous but it is important.

Dear Mr. Smith:

This will confirm that <Your Firm> ("YF") has the sole and exclusive right to sell the business and related real property owned by you, ABC Corporation (the "Company"), which right commences upon your acceptance of this letter, and is authorized to act as the sole and exclusive representative of the Company in seeking to arrange and negotiate the sale of all or substantially all of its assets (the "Transaction") on terms and conditions acceptable to you.

The duties to be performed by YF shall be divided into two phases:
- Phase I: Business profiling, identifying appropriate purchasers and quantifying of prospective purchaser's opinions of value and probable transaction structures and
- Phase II: Collection and preparation of confidential materials to be used in presenting the Company to prospective purchaser, developing the Business Presentation Report or Prospectus, marketing, identifying and qualifying of prospective purchasers, negotiation and closing.

During Phase I, which shall commence on the date of your acceptance hereof and shall be completed in approximately four weeks, YF shall prepare a Market Place Position and Summary of Values Report. This Report will contain data and information regarding the Company's current and potential value as viewed by potential investors and will provide the basis for developing a Marketing Plan, Business Development Plan or other such Plan as you may deem appropriate. Your decision to proceed to Phase II will be evidenced by your executing an Authorization to Commence Marketing document.

Phase II shall be for a period of twelve months, commencing on the date of your Authorization to Commence Marketing. At that time, we would also agree on the proposed price and terms of sale in a separate agreement. During Phase II, YF agrees to prepare and initiate the Marketing Plan, attempt to find prospective purchasers for the Company, to participate in negotiations respecting said Transaction, to do all else YF deems reasonably necessary and within its capabilities to assist the Company in attempting to effect said Transaction.

YF agrees to present such information in a manner and form reasonably acceptable to the Company, subject to any requirements imposed by law and protocol as to manner and form of presentation.

For our services in connection with Phase I, the Company shall pay YF a Retainer and Financial Advisory Fee of $_____. The Retainer and Financial Advisory Fee shall be credited against the Transaction Fee which is fully earned by YF if the Transaction or similar Transaction to that contemplated under Phase II is consummated during Phase I or Phase II (including any extensions) or within eighteen months thereafter with a purchaser (corporation, partnership, individuals, member(s) of Company management, family members, etc.) with whom YF and/or the Company has had discussions relating to the Transaction during Phase I or Phase II (including any extensions thereof).

The Company agrees to pay the balance of the Transaction Fee to YF by certified check at the closing of the Transaction according to the following formula:

__% of the value of the first $500,000 of Total Consideration, plus

__% of the value of the second $500,000, plus

__% of the value of the third $1,000,000,

__% of the value of the fourth $1,000,000,

__% of the value of the fifth $1,000,000,

__% of the value in excess of $4,000,000.

Total Consideration, for purposes of this Agreement, shall be defined as, but not limited to, any cash, securities, credit arrangements, assumption of Company liabilities, assets, promissory notes, face value of obligations arising from employment agreements, covenants not to compete, and lease contracts for the amount above fair market value; other property owned or controlled by the Company, its officers or shareholders, and any other like arrangements intended to convey value in connection with the Transaction.

The Company agrees that once electing to proceed with Phase II, if it decides not to sell the Company, or if the Company or its owners take some action which would prevent YF from selling the Company or consummating the Transaction, the Company shall pay YF promptly, upon written notice from YF, $_____ per month from the date of inception of Phase II as full consideration for services rendered under Phase II and as liquidated damages, it being acknowledged that YF will have conferred upon the Company a benefit in the form of advisory and other services which may be difficult to value.

The Company recognizes and confirms that in representing its interest in effecting the above Transaction, YF will be using and relying on information and data furnished to YF by the Company, and YF does not assume responsibility for the accuracy and completeness of the information. YF will not undertake to independently verify the information, and will not make an appraisal of any of the individual assets of the Company.

The Company represents that all information to be furnished in connection with the proposed transaction is true and complete in all material respects and contains no material omissions. The Company agrees to hold YF harmless against all losses, claims, damages, liabilities, and expenses including reasonable attorneys' fees which YF may incur or which may be asserted against YF as a result of the breach or alleged breach of the foregoing representation.

The Company agrees that should it appear to YF that there will not be sufficient funds to pay YF's Transaction Fee, such obligation shall be paid by the purchaser instead of the Company at the closing and the purchasing price and down payment to be paid by the purchaser shall be reduced accordingly.

The parties hereto acknowledge that YF is not licensed as a securities broker or dealer by any state or federal government agency; accordingly, the Company shall not seek to have YF become involved in the sale or offering for sale of the Company's shares of stock. In the event that YF introduces a prospect for the purchase of the assets of the Company, and the Company and the prospect subsequently agree that the prospect will purchase the shares of stock of the Company rather than its assets, the parties hereto agree that (1) YF is entitled to its full Transaction Fee as agreed herein for the purchase of assets and (2) the Company shall not seek to defeat the right of YF to its fee earned pursuant to this Agreement by raising the defense or claim that YF brought about the sale of the Company shares of stock rather than its assets.

The Company agrees that upon consummation of the Transaction, YF may, at its expense, announce to the business community through the Wall Street Journal and other appropriate media its role in effecting the transaction.

By your signature below, you confirm that you are duly authorized to enter into this Agreement on behalf of the Company.

Sincerely yours,

<Your Company>

_____   _____
<Name>   Date

CONFIRMED AND ACCEPTED:

_____   _____
President   Date

and ALL SHAREHOLDERS
          Per Cent (%)
          Shares
Name   Outstanding   Date

_____

_____

_____

Authorization to
Commence Marketing Effort

By this addendum <YOUR FIRM> is authorized to commence efforts to sell that
business known as: (Company)

located at

Proposed Terms of Sale:

      Down Payment $ _____ includes Transaction Fee of $ _____
                                                   Description

      Assumable Debt $ _____
      Other $ _____
      Balance by Note $ _____ Seller will carry balance at $
                                         per month including ____% interest on
                                       unpaid balance, secured by assets being
                                       sold and personal guarantee of buyer.
      Total Purchase Price $ _____ includes Transaction Fee of $_____

Inventory:
Approximate Inventory at time of sale, valued at cost, to be included in Total Purchase
Price: $_____. (The Down Payment or Notes to Seller will be adjusted by any
variance.)
Not Included in Sale:

Covenants:
      Owner(s) agree not to compete with purchaser in a similar business
      for _____ months within a _____ mile radius of the company location.
      Owner agrees to train purchaser for a period of _____ days as part
      of the purchase price.
Lease:
      Owner warrants the transferability of the existing lease or a new
      lease at $ _____ per month for _____ remaining months and
      _____ renewal option(s) of _____ years.

This Addendum is part of that Marketing Agreement dated _____

Owner _____ Date _____

ABC Corporation
123 Any Street
Yourcity, XZ 00000

Date

Dear XXXXX:

In accordance with our telephone conversation of this morning we submit the following for your review. If this meets with your understanding and approval please so indicate by your signature below.

I, the undersigned, hereby engage The Burbank Group, Inc. (BG) to prepare a business valuation on the business known as ABC Corporation. In return for this service it is understood and agreed that BG will receive a Financial Advisory Fee in the amount of Five Thousand Dollars, $5,000 payable upon execution of this Agreement.

I recognize and confirm that BG will be using and relying on information and data furnished to BG by me and BG does not assume responsibility for the accuracy or completeness of the information and that BG will not make an appraisal of any of the individual assets of the business. I represent and warrant that all information to be furnished is true and complete in all material respects and contains no material omissions. I agree to hold BG harmless against all claims, demands, or causes of action arising out of the use of the information provided and the Business Valuation generated therefrom.

I have read, understand and hereby agree to the above terms and provisions of this Agreement and hereby acknowledge receipt of a copy. Also, I represent and warrant that the undersigned constitute all of the owners/partners/shareholders of the above Business and hereby personally guarantee performance of this Agreement.

Agreed to and understood:

_____   Date

for Your Firm, Inc.

XXXXXXXXX, CBI   Date

CORPORATE RESOLUTION
OF AUTHORITY

I, _____

hereby certify that I am the duly elected and qualified Clerk/Secretary of

_____, a lawful corporation in the

(JURISDICTION), and have custody of the official records of said corporation and that

the following is a true copy of the resolution adopted by the Board of Directors thereof at

a meeting of the Board duly called and held on _____, at which a quorum

was present, and that such resolution is now in full force and effect.

RESOLVED: That the _____ and

_____ are/is hereby authorized to sign any and all lawful

documents necessary to list, transfer and/or sell the real estate, fixtures, goodwill,

trademarks, trade names, leasehold rights, equipment and inventory. I further certify

that the foregoing resolution conforms to all applicable provisions of the by-laws of said

corporation relative to such a transaction, and the party/parties named herein are

empowered to act for this corporation as provided herein. In witness thereof I have

hereunto set my signature and affixed the corporate seal this _____ day of _____

2____.

_____

Clerk/Secretary

I _____, a director of said corporation hereby confirm
the correctness of the contents of the foregoing certificate.

_____

Director

Name
Business Name
Address
City, State, Zip

Date

Financial Advisory Agreement

Dear <Salutation>,

This will confirm that <Business Name> (Company), hereby engages <Your Firm> (YF) to prepare a Marketplace Position and Summary of Values report for the Company.

THE ASSIGNMENT:
YF agrees to provide the following services to Company as described below.

- Profile Company's past and present operating performance and obtain an understanding of future operating prospects.
- Analyze Company's past and present financial statements and prepare projections as may be required to predict future results including recasting, ratio analysis, industry comparison (when applicable) and analysis of all financial and operating information.
- Develop a Marketplace Position and Summary of Values report for review by the Company.
- Provide advisory services to Company, its accounting firm and legal advisors regarding transaction structuring and related matters as may be required to prepare Company for sale or merger

HOLD HARMLESS:
I/we recognize and confirm that YF will be using and relying on information and data furnished by Company and YF does not assume responsibility for the accuracy or completeness of the information and that YF will not make an appraisal of any of the individual assets of the business. I/we represent and warrant that all information to be furnished is true and complete in all material respects and contains no material omissions. I/we agree to hold YF harmless against all claims, demands, or causes of action arising out of the use of information provided and the report generated therefrom.

COMPENSATION:
In return for this service it is understood and agreed that YF will receive a Retainer and Advisory Fee in the amount of ($XXXXXX), one half ($XXXXX) payable upon execution of this agreement and the balance due upon completion of the report.

(Optional) It is further understood and agreed that in the event that YF is engaged to market Company, the Retainer and Financial Advisory Fee will be credited against the transaction fee earned by YF.

I/we have read, understood and hereby agree to the above terms and provisions of this Agreement and hereby acknowledge receipt of a copy. Also, I/we represent and warrant that the undersigned constitute all of the owners, partners, and shareholders of Company and hereby personally guarantee performance of this Agreement.

If you are in agreement with the above, please signify by your signature below.

Very truly yours,

Your Name
Title

I/we have read, understand and agree to the terms of the above Agreement.

By <Client Signature>   Date

Required Information

#	Description	
1	• **Financial and Legal** • Financial statements (prior 5 yrs if available) o Balance Sheets o Income Statement • Tax returns (prior 5 yrs) • Breakdown of sales by month (prior 3 yrs) • Breakdown of sales and expenses by month since last financial statement and/or tax return (each month for current year) • Annual sales for top 10 customers (prior 3 yrs)……………..	
2	• **Product/Service** • Segmentation of sales by product/service…………………… • Target Profit Gross Margin by segment (by product/service) • Volume by segment (annual basis)……...	
3	• **Assets** • List of Furniture, Fixtures, and Equipment (FF&E) with your estimate of Fair Market Value (FMV) • Estimated values of FMV inventory at time of sale	
4	• **Staff** • List of key employees by first name, tenure, function, wage/salary, # hours worked • Number of employees by position/function • Description of employee benefits, major benefit policies	
5	• **Premises** • Leased property - Copy of premise lease and addendums • Owned property – description of each building, purpose, age, square footage, copy of plot plan, deed, recent tax bill, environmental issues, type of building (metal, brick, etc.), # parking spaces • List restrictions of building codes and/or zoning laws (if any) • List of any liens on properties (if any)	
6	• **Industry Information** • Industry related information relating to outlook, operating ratios, trends and market conditions -- often found in trade journals, etc • List of major trade journals • Copy of Company promotional materials	

Thank you

Your Name, FCBI

Business Profile and
Buyer Identification
Workbook

Your Firm
Address
Contact information

Business Profile

Business Name _____
Address _____
City _____ State _____ Zip Code _____
Business Phone _____ Facsimile _____
Cell Phone _____ Email _____
Home Address _____
City/Town _____ State _____ Zip Code _____
Home Phone _____

Form of Ownership:
Individual _____ Partnership _____ #Partners _____ S Corp. _____ or C Corp. _____

Partners/Shareholders Names   % ownership or #Shares

_____
_____
_____
_____
_____
_____
_____

Location:
Is there a Lease? Yes _____ No _____

Current lease has _____ months remaining at $_____ per month with option to renew for

an additional period of _____ years. Current Lease expires on ___ / ___ / ___

Option to renew expires on ___ / ___ / ___ # Options _____

Rent under: Option 1 $_____/ Month Option 2 $_____/ Month Option 3 $_____/ Month

Does lease contain option to buy Real Estate? Yes _____ No _____

If owned and to be included in sale need copies of: Deed ___ Tax bill ____ and Plot plan _____

Landlord's Name _____

Address_____

Telephone # _____ Is Lease assignable? ____ New Lease available? _____

What is the rent per square foot next door? _____ Across the street? _____

Parking: # cars _____ In lot _____ On street _____

History

Date founded _____ and/or date acquired _____
If acquired, the price paid was $ _____
Total down payment was _____ Note was _____
Security for note was _____

Give a brief overview of the company from its founding to the present. Note major changes and stages in its evolution to its present structure. Use additional sheet if required.

The Business:

Describe this business:

Hours/Days Open:

Square footage business occupies:

Number of seats (if applicable):   Number of shifts:

Special licenses required?   Vending contracts?

Assets
Owner's estimate of Values, Orderly Liquidation Value (OLV) and Average Age of:

	Orderly Liquidation	**Replacement Value**	**Age/Condition**
Furnishings, Fixtures and Equipment (FFE)			
Leasehold Improvements			
Inventory			
Vehicle(s)			
Patents, Franchises, Licenses etc.			
Accounts Receivable			
Other			
Totals			

Provide a list of all assets to be transferred. Include serial numbers where available.

Staff

Family
Number of family members active in Business: Full-time_____ Part-time_____ List below:

Name	Job Description	PT FT	Pay Rate	Hours/Wk	Stay or Leave

Non Family
Number of non-family employees: Full-time___ Part-time _____

Name	Job Description	PT FT	Pay Rate	Hours/Wk	Stay or Leave

Benefits provided and cost per employee

Employee employment contracts? If yes provide a copy of same:

Copy of W-2s and 1099s for latest tax year:

What is the status of the labor pool for the company?

Is the company unionized?   If not, is unionization likely in the future?

How much of your industry is unionized?

Operations

How much would you have to pay a manager in order to run this business "absentee"?

$_____

What percentage of supplies or inventory would be considered dead or obsolete? _____%

As a new owner, how long would it take to be functional in this business? _____

From start up, how long to reach current level of profitability? (months) _____

How accurately can you predict revenues? (explain)

How much training is required to perform and understand this company's operations?

How important is the owner to the revenues of this business?

Explain how new business is obtained: (Owners influence, walk in, direct mail, etc.)

What special license, degree or skills would a new owner need?

Does the business have room for expansion?

Owner's Background:
Owner's background prior to founding or acquisition:

Education

Special skills or interests

Prior positions held

Owner's duties and hours devoted to each per week

Personnel Management		Customer service	
Administration		Sales/Marketing	
Production		Financial Mgmt	
Other			

Sales Segmentation

How do you price your product/service?

Details of sales and target gross profit by segment:

Segment	Volume/Revenue	Target Gross Profit

Have there been recent price changes?

Customer Base

List the top10 customers by volume for the past three years:

Year		Year		Year	
Customer	Volume	Customer	Volume	Customer	Volume

Describe your typical customer.

What other industries, businesses or customers could you serve?

Have you lost any significant customers/accounts in the past two years? If so why?

Do you expect to loose any significant customers/accounts in the future? If so why?

Competitors

Name	Major Strength/Weakness	Distance

How many competitors have gone out of business in the last three years and why?

Does your industry have a trade association(s)? Include name(s) and contact information.

What is the outlook for your industry?

Government Regulations

Are there anticipated or actual changes in government regulations that will impact your business?

Environmental

Are there environmental risks or hazardous materials used in or by this business? If so provide details.

Do you produce anything that is considered hazardous? If so provide details.

Liability

How common are lawsuits within your industry?

What do the lawsuits generally entail?

Do you have product/professional liability insurance?   How have the premiums been trending?

Do you have any pending litigation?

Sales and Marketing

What efforts do you expend to grow the business?

What do you need to grow the business further?

Equipment

Staff

Financial

Other

Liens/Debts/Encumbrances

Lender	Amount	Collateral

Miscellaneous

Copies of pension/profit sharing plans
Declaration pages of all insurance policies
Copies of independent party reports:
    Copies of OSHA reviews and reports
    Copies of environmental audits or reports
    Copies of sales, state, and federal tax reviews, audits or reports

Advisors

Name	Address	Telephone and Facsimile	Email
Attorney			
Accountant			
Insurance Agent			
Other			

FIXTURES, FURNITURE
& EQUIPMENT LIST

Company:

Quantity	Item	Serial/Model Number

Chapter Eleven

Marketing Tools

One of life's most intimidating challenges is to be faced with a blank piece of paper and be expected to write something intelligent upon it. The pressure seems to increase when you realize the resulting document will bear your name.

We have compiled a sampling of letters, post cards and flyers to assist you in attracting clients. You probably will notice the main theme of these mailers is not primarily to sell businesses. All of the samples have been tried and tested. For best results you should plan to follow up on the mailing with a phone call.

Fifty mailings a week for beginners seems to be about right. The number mailed each week could be reduced as activity increased but we found twenty should be mailed each week no matter what.

The best way to assure consistency in your mailing efforts is to outsource or delegate the actual mechanics of producing, stuffing, stamping and mailing to another. We hired a special assistant whose only job was to sustain the mailing effort for the entire staff.

The assistant maintained the associate's individual database of target companies to whom he would mail something four times per year. Six hundred fifty names are required by associates mailing fifty pieces each week (52 wks / 4 mailings = 13 weeks X 50 pieces = 650) and two hundred sixty by those mailing twenty per week. We purchased a high speed laser printer (20 pages per minute) to support the assistant in producing mailings for the staff of twenty or so associates.

Associates also developed databases of names of referral sources to which mailings were sent at least four times per year. These mailings typically were either examples of current opportunities or recent sales. A majority of our buyers and many of our sellers came to us as a result of this activity.

Sample letter #1

<Date>

Dear <salutation>:

Are you increasing your business's value or are you just making money?

You know how to make money with your business. We know how to make it more valuable. Our experience may be especially valuable to you if you are considering the sale of your business now or within the next five years.

We have assisted more than 2,000 companies maximize their business's value, either for their own or their children's benefit. If your business is one of your largest assets and you want to secure and/or increase your business's worth (not necessarily by making more profits) then it will be worthwhile for us to discuss this further. No obligations and in confidence, of course.

My direct, private line is XXX-VVV-NNNN. It would be helpful to alert your secretary to expect my call so I may follow up with you.

Warmest regards,

Your Name

Sample letter #2

Date

Business Owner
Business Name
Address
City, State, Zip

Dear Business Owner:

Peter Druker is quoted as saying ***"The best way to predict the future is to create it."***
Are you planning to pass your business on to family? Considering the sale of your business?
Creating value while earning profits? No matter what your answer, we can help you increase
the value of your business. Our clients are owners of small and mid-size companies (businesses
with sales from $100,000 to $20 million). Specifically, business owners who want to create
value in their business, either for their own benefit or to advantage their children.

We can help you:
- Acquire the ability to increase your company's present value by two to six times
  (without increasing declared profits).
- Learn how to run your business so you can cash out in style.
- Create a succession plan for your business and an exit plan for you.
- Control your company's ultimate destiny and increase your wealth.

Give us a call. No obligation and in confidence, of course (XXX) XXX-XXXX.

Sincerely,

VVV BBBBBB, CBI, CBC
President

Sample letter #3

Business Owner
Business Name
Address
City, State, Zip

Dear Business Owner:

Ever wonder if your company could command the Big Money you hear that other business owners have received for theirs? Somehow, the owners of those companies created value beyond profits.

Would you believe that:

- A Shrewsbury firm with $50,000 in assets showing a **$50,000 loss sold for $495,000.00 in CASH?**

- A Southbridge company with a book value of $156,000 and pre-tax earnings of $26,000 sold for **ONE MILLION THREE HUNDRED FIFTY THOUSAND DOLLARS?**

- One Worcester family increased the value of its company by **FOUR MILLION DOLLARS** without showing any significant increase in earnings or book value?

Are you planning to pass your business on to family? Considering the sale of your business? Creating value while earning profits? No matter what your answer, we can help you increase the value of your business. Our clients are owners of small and mid-size companies. Specifically, business owners who want to create value in their business, either for their own benefit or their children's benefit.

We want to help you create value in your business and, when the time is right, <u>Cash Out on Your Terms</u>. For more information, give us a call. No obligation and in confidence, of course. ZZZ XXX-CCCC.

Sincerely,

XYZ ZZZZOOM
President

◆ WHAT <u>COULD</u> YOUR BUSINESS BE WORTH?

◆ ARE YOU BUILDING "REAL VALUE"?

A 20 Second Quiz for Successful Business People *Only* ...

On the Other Side!

Do you know...

	Do you know...	Yes	No
1.	If you are building wealth or just making money?	☐	☐
2.	How to increase Value without increasing profits?	☐	☐
3.	What the business is worth today or could be worth tomorrow?	☐	☐
4.	Why some businesses sell for Big Bucks and others do not?	☐	☐
5.	When to Cash Out so you can Cash In?	☐	☐

SCORE (# Yes's):

4-5 Congratulations! When you want to cash out, you should be able
     to with **lots of money!**

0-3 **Caution!** You are probably working really hard but **may not end up
     with as much cash** as you think.

Contact us to find out more.
Your Firm, Inc. Joe Salesman
Telephone 111 222-3333 Joe@YourFirm.com
Building and Obtaining Value for Family Businesses

Marketplace Position and Summary of Values

You receive much more than a Business Valuation

This unique report provides Private and Family Businesses with the same Strategic Planning Tools Public Companies *expect* and Private Businesses *deserve*.

When you finish reading your report you not only know the real value of your business but you also have:

> Valuable Strategic Planning Tools
> Value Enhancement Recommendations
> A description of your Ideal Acquirer (for when the time comes)
> Estimated Fair Cash Value
> Estimated Fair Market Value, and Probable Transaction Structure

Strategic Planning Tools
Understand how to build VALUE in addition to profits
Benchmark your business practices compared with those of others in your industry
Identify opportunities for improvement

Value Enhancement Recommendations
Specific recommendations to enhance the value of the enterprise
Gain control of business's value
Ability to include value enhancement considerations in future decisions

Description of Ideal Buyer/Investor
Gain an understanding of the different buyers in today's marketplace, what they will pay and why
Preserve confidentiality and value by limiting marketplace exposure
Only "right buyers" who pay "right prices" need be introduced to the company
Reduce possibility of becoming shop worn

Fair Cash Value
Understand how asset values, cash flows, bank financing and business environment combine to produce a cash price
Provide basis for consideration of seller participation in financing a transaction

Fair Market Value (by ASA* definition includes seller financing)
Ability to compare cash price with a price where seller provides some financing
Make an informed decision to participate based upon amount involved and quality of the buyer *
American Society of Appraisers

Transaction Structuring
Identify structure best suited to minimizing tax impact (It's not what you get but what
you get to keep that's important)
Structure the transaction so the business will stay sold
Construct a win win transaction

Summary
With a (Your Firm)**"Marketplace Position and Summary of Values"** report for your business you
will know how to:

Gain control of your company's value
Build value in addition to earning profits
Make decisions designed to increase value as well as profits
Sell your business for the most money quickly and quietly when the time comes
View your business from the outside in
Understand factors that drive your company's value
Enjoy the ability to control and grow your company's worth while increasing profits
Gain insight to your company's value based upon experience acquired in over 2,000 transactions
Be able to structure a transaction that increases value, minimizes taxes and risks

As you can see, you get *more than just a Business Valuation* when (Your Firm) develops a
"Marketplace Position and Summary of Values" survey for your business.

Reports include a complete text summarizing the results of a comprehensive business and financial
analyses that explain:

Financial statement and balance sheet adjustments
Projections, ratio analysis
Risk analysis
Bankability analysis
Justification of purchase price
Probable transaction structure and
Comparison with industry

This report is often used for mergers and acquisitions as much of the "due diligence" necessary for the
acquisition of a company is accomplished in the process of valuation.

Your Firm
Your Address
Your Town , XX   51545
555 555-5555

The
Burbank Group
Intermediaries

Since 1979

Business
Available for
Acquisition

Type Business: Injection Molding - Established 45 years

Location: Central New England

Financial:

Year	2000	2001	2003
Revenues	2,345,000	2,266,220	2,456,000
Adj. EBIT	245K	265K	325K

Market Served: Thd rted zxitr uudfu ikbnf jjudrty bfikdrry strvving sdrihjk jklifd f eebne hrejh wenhy

Marketing Area: Thd rted zxitr uudfu ikbnf jjudrty bfikdrry strvving sdrihjk jklifd f eebne hrejh wenhy

Customer Concentrations: Thd rted zxitr uudfu ikbnf jjudrty bfikdrry strvving sdrihjk jklifd f eebne hrejh wenhy

Facilities and Equipment: Thd rted zxitr uudfu ikbnf jjudrty bfikdrry strvving sdrihjk jklifd f eebne hrejh wenhy

Competition: Thd rted zxitr uudfu ikbnf jjudrty bfikdrry strvving sdrihjk jklifd f eebne hrejh wenhy

The Opportunity: Thd rted zxitr uudfu ikbnf jjudrty bfikdrry strvving sdrihjk jklifd f eebne hrejh wenhy. Thd rted zxitr uudfu ikbnf jjudrty bfikdrry strvving sdrihjk jklifd f eebne hrejh wenhy hyhd rted zxitr uudfu ikbnf jjudrty bfikdrry strvving sdrihjk jklifd f eebne hrejh wenhy

For additional information contact:
Attractive Salesperson
Your Firm, Inc.
Your Town and Address
Your telephone and email etc.

## Chapter Twelve

Wealth Creation Strategies
for Small and Mid-Size Companies

The Wall Street or Two Step approach to selling businesses will occasionally present opportunities for Buy Side assignments with those business owners wishing to expand through acquisitions.

Growth through acquisition should not be considered an option reserved solely for large or Public Companies. Small and mid-size businesses that opt to grow by acquiring other companies, rather than growing one new customer at a time, can gain benefits in addition to increased sales and profits.

Our unique understanding of marketplace dynamics that increase valuation multiples can be enormously valuable to owners of Private companies. Because few business owners really know what their business is worth, even fewer focus on creating and building value in their business. Most business owners are not creating wealth through their companies, rather, they are only making money. We can help change that.

Timing is Right
Two elements have combined making growth through acquisition an attractive option for small and middle market companies.

Demographics - The maturing of the Baby Boom generation, many of whom own their own businesses, will increase the number of owners willing to consider selling to an historic high.

Financing - Money is available to finance small and middle market acquisitions. Banks and non-traditional lenders are aggressively pursuing acquisition lending at a level we have not seen in twenty years. Cash required to consummate a transaction is at an all time low.

Profit Pays the Bills

Profit and Value are two main financial components of every business. Profits are essential and therefore on every businessperson's front burner. Value, on the other hand, is an elusive and intangible issue. Unlike public company presidents, whose effectiveness is measured daily in their firm's share price, private and family business presidents need not be concerned with their company's value as their shareholders, if any, typically focus upon profit only.

Value Measures the Size of Your Pile

Shareholders of Public Companies measure their wealth (or the size of their pile) using share value not earnings per share. Successful CEOs, therefore, develop strategic plans for growth and profit that maximize shareholders' value. Mergers and Acquisitions is a fundamental element of most strategic plans to increase profits and value simultaneously.

What follows is an overview of public company strategies to increase profits and value through acquisitions and how to adapt these strategies to private and family businesses. Although the topic may seem technical and complex it is really quite basic and straightforward.

An Overview

Adding earnings or profits is self-explanatory. We will, therefore, focus primarily on the value component of growth through acquisitions.

We know a public company's Price/Earnings Ratio measures the amount investors are willing to pay for $1 of company earnings and that a P/E ratio of 15 for a well-run company is not unusual. Consequently, company BIG with 100 million dollars of earnings and a P/E Ratio of 15 has a value of 1.5 billion dollars. We also know private company P/E Ratios are much lower than those of public companies.

Strategy #1 Acquire companies with a smaller P/E ratio than yours
Example:
The Transaction - Company BIG with a P/E Ratio of 15 acquires company SMALLER and pays 10 times earnings (P/E ratio = 10). Company SMALLER's 10 million dollars of earnings are added to those of company BIG.

Increases in Value Calculation - SMALLER's earnings are now worth 15X instead of 10 times earnings resulting in an immediate increase in value of 5X earnings or $50,000,000 (5 times $10,000,000) over and above the value paid by company BIG.

Strategy #2 Reduce expenses through economies of scale
The picture gets even better if eliminating duplications and other economies of

scale will reduce company SMALLER's expenses. Every dollar reduction in expenses translates into $15 of value (P/E Ratio of 15 X $1).

Increases in Value Calculation - Company BIG is able to eliminate 1 million dollars of redundant expense. $1,000,000 X 15 = $15 million dollar increase in value.

Strategy #3 Acquire according to a strategic plan
BIG's acquisition of a company in order to gain specific benefits such as proprietary products, technology, channels of distribution or talent base for example, can result in an improved outlook for company BIG. Whereas the P/E ratio usually reflects expectations of future profits, a strategic acquisition often produces a P/E ratio increase. In this example company BIG's P/E ratio increases by a dollar from 15X to 16 times earnings after the acquisition was announced.

Increases in Value Calculation - Every point increase in company BIG's P/E ratio equates to 111 million dollars of added value (original $100 million in earnings plus addition of SMALLER's $10 million plus $1 million in reduced expenses times 1).

Calculation of Increased Value to Shareholders:

In the above example, company BIG's acquisition of company SMALLER not only has increased earnings by $10 million but has increased company BIG's value as follows.

- Increased value of $10 million in earnings $ 50,000,000
- Reduced SMALLER's expenses by $1 million   15,000,000
- Increase of BIG's P/E Ratio from 15 to 16   111,000,000
- Total increase in SIZE of PILE (VALUE) $176,000,000

This CEO has made the kind of a deal that makes shareholders happy.

No wonder there is so much M&A activity in the marketplace. A well conceived acquisition should produce wondrous results. These dynamics are not reserved exclusively for public companies. Private and family businesses can and should take advantage of the opportunities presented by growth through acquisitions. We will now apply these principles to smaller businesses and analyze the results.

Value Building Strategies for Small and Middle Market Businesses

Private companies can employ the same three strategies used in the above public company example given an understanding of a few basic principles.

General Principles:
Financial
Small companies generally have small P/E ratios. P/E ratios increase as companies grow and develop structure. P/E ratios increase as dependency upon the owner decreases.

Valuation Principles
Two major value determiners are:

- Perception of risk and

- Expectation of future profit

Businesses with essentially identical earnings, therefore, can have widely diverse values.

"Round Ball" Principle - Non Financial
None of us are equally talented in all directions. We are not round balls, footballs or Frisbees perhaps, but no one can "do it all" well. Company strengths and weaknesses will therefore generally mirror those of its owner. Armed with a basic understanding of the ground rules we can begin to formulate a strategic plan to grow and build wealth through acquisitions. Table A summarizes P/E ratios, level of earnings, definition of earnings and management style by company size. We can use Table A for reference as we develop our plan.

	P/E Ratio	Usual level of Earnings and Definition of Earnings	Type of Management
Wall Street	15X to OMG*	Typically measured in millions Definition of Earnings: After Tax * Oh My God	Professional management with many levels of responsibility. Management's objective is to maximize profits and value to satisfy stockholder demands.
Middle Market	3 to 15X	$500.000 to small millions Definition of Earnings: Pre/after tax and various EBITs unless the company represents a unique opportunity, (proprietary product, technology, channels of distribution, talent base etc.), the all cash, high multiple Wall Street price is unattainable. Otherwise, dynamics found when selling Upper Main Street apply.	Segmentation of responsibilities and management structure well defined. Owner may or may not be involved in operations to a significant degree.
Upper Main Street	3 to 7X	More than $100,000 but less than $500,000 Definition of Earnings: Adjusted EBIT - Earnings Before Interest, Taxes plus Depreciation and Adjustments (less an Appropriate Manager's salary)	Owner still major element of company's success. Levels of responsibilities and management structure are evolving.
Main Street	1 to 4X	Typically 100K, more or less Definition of Earnings: Discretionary Earnings - Dollars available for new owner's compensation, acquisition debt service, actual depreciation reserves and return on invested capital.	Owner is vital to operations. "Wears all the hats" - little to no management depth.

Develop your Plan

The plan should begin with an honest assessment of your company's strengths, weaknesses and the opportunities your business and industry represent. Picture a bell curve representing your company's strength and weaknesses. The top of the curve represents what has gotten you where you are. The outer extremes represent areas of opportunity. Your ideal acquisition should be a firm whose bell curve is the inverse of yours and by acquisition, both companies benefit.

Example:
Your areas of strength are:

- Quality workmanship
- On time delivery
- Good management with
- Excellent systems and controls plus
- A loyal customer base

Areas of opportunity are:

- Need quality sales force
- Additional capabilities along with
- Competent personnel and
- Access to new customer base

Assume for this example that you own a printing company with annual revenues of 10 million dollars. Your specialty is high speed black and white 81/2 X 11 with some spot color. You produce manuals and provide forms management services for the computer industry and others. However, you serve predominantly high tech companies.

You develop a plan to acquire a smaller printer with a quality sales and work force serving a completely different customer base. You decide the company should provide the color and graphic design capabilities your firm lacks and the company should represent opportunity for improvement through upgraded systems, controls and stronger management.

Even if you are on the right track
you'll get run over if you just sit there.

Will Rogers

Further Define and Search

Online and other computer databases make finding your acquisition easier than ever. Additional search criteria usually includes:

- Geographic area
- Number of employees
- Annual sales or revenues
- Specific SIC # for type business sought
- Single or multiple locations

Once your list of possible acquisitions is completed the fun part of mailing, calling, visiting and touring, negotiating and finally completing the transaction can begin. You can attempt doing the job yourself or you can engage professional intermediaries to act as your in house M&A department.

The Transaction and the Benefit

You had your firm valued prior to the acquisition and determined a value of $7,500,000 (P/E ratio of 7.5 with an Adjusted EBIT of $1,000,000) - Size of your pile = $7,500,000.

You acquire a firm that fits your criteria with $3 million in revenues and an Adjusted EBIT of $400,000. You pay 4 times Adjusted EBIT or $1,600,000. Improved systems and controls plus elimination of redundant expenses increased income $100,000. After the acquisition the combined firms develop a P/E multiple of 10.

Calculate Increase in Size of Pile (Value)

In the above example, the acquisition not only has increased earnings by $500,000 ($400,000 in earnings plus 100,000 in cost reductions) but has increased the combined company's value as follows:

Value

New multiple of 10 X combined earnings of $1,500,00	15,000,000
Old Value of 7.5MM plus Acquisition Value of 1.6MM	9,100,000
Total Increase in SIZE of PILE (VALUE)	$5,900,000

Improvements in management, capabilities, sales force and customer base plus the ability to cross sell printing should further enable the combined company to increase sales, profits and value even further.

Do It Again

Management determines that if all of the mailing and fulfillment jobs the combined company now farms out (about $300,000/yr) are brought in house, earnings would increase and additional customers attracted to the combined company for the same reasons mentioned above. A small mailing service with $750,000 in revenue and $150,000 in earnings is purchased for $450,000 or a P/E ratio of 3. Management calculates earnings to increase from $150,000 to $215,000 with the addition of their $300,000 of volume and small economies of scale.

Management calculates an increase in value of the $750,000 purchase as follows: Purchased earnings @ $150,000 plus added earnings of $65,000 from work previously outsourced produces $215,000 in earnings to be added to the combined company's earnings.

Calculate Increase in Value

Earnings of $215,000 multiplied by Combined companies P/E ratio of 10 produces a new VALUE of ($215,000 X 10) $2,150,000. New value of $2,150,000 less price paid of $750,000 produces an increase in value of $1,400,000.

This acquisition added $215,000 in earnings but produces an increase in the size of the pile (value) by $1,400,000.

Summary

Let's measure the height of the pile after applying these Growth Through Acquisition principles.

Value of original company	$7,500,000
Benefit of first acquisition	5,900,000
Benefit of second acquisition	1,400,000
Total Pile (Value)	$15,800,000

The principles outlined here work regardless of the present size of your client's business although the larger the business the easier it is to achieve dramatic results.

Sample Report #1

The fee for this type report usually ranges between $1,500 and $5,000

Marketplace Position and Summary of Values

Produced especially for

Client Company

Prepared by:
TTTTTT, CBI
LLLLLLLL, LLC.
Telephone XXX.794-1200
Facsimile XXX.794-1042

Table of Contents

Sections

INTRODUCTION

This report has been prepared to accompany the presentation of The Burbank Group's work to date on behalf of Your Client, Inc. and is submitted to the company's ownership for review and approval in preparation for possible sale of the company. The Report is based on data and information provided by management. Results and conclusions can be no more accurate than this data and information allow.

This presentation, and accompanying data, are to be used as tools to:
- provide a marketplace view of this company
- understand this company's uniqueness, and the opportunity it represents
- identify the means for positioning the company so as to obtain the highest and best
- value
- develop an effective marketing plan built around the company's uniqueness
- determine what specific steps should be taken to further prepare the business for sale

The Report is organized to cover essential information regarding the following major areas of concern:

A Business Analysis - an investigation of balance sheet, income statement, operating data, and industry information; so as to quantify the elements most likely to be considered when determining worth. These include values of tangible assets, historic and projected earnings and cash flows, and perception or risk.

The Marketplace and Valuations - definitions of value, an overview of the current marketplace for privately held businesses, an identification of probable kinds of acquirers for this business, a discussion of the techniques and approaches most likely to be used by the marketplace in establishing worth, and a summary of the values which result from the application of this thinking.

Transaction Structuring and Plan - a determination of the kinds of acquirers to be targeted, and the highest value they are likely to perceive. Discussion will also include an indication of the supporting data which is to be gathered and prepared as part of the marketing effort. Lastly, strategy and planning should identify probable elements of the sale transaction - elements such as non-compete agreements, down payment and the role of financing.

It must be clear that the validity of all of the information referenced above is limited in time. Market conditions and input data can cause conclusions and values to change. The duration over which this kind of information is valid depends heavily upon this business, its industry, and general economic conditions. Timely documentation of input data provides the means for determining whatever change might have taken place.

This report has been developed solely for Client Company and will not be presented to Investors.

For tax or legal advice, we encourage you to consult your accountant and/or attorney. Such advice must be based on your individual situation and, therefore, be given by a qualified professional.

DATA SOURCES
All information describing the company has been obtained through interviews with the firm's owners, and from the company's books, records, and accountant's statements. Data regarding the industry, marketplace, and economy within which the company operates, has been obtained from:
· Annual Statement Studies - Robert Morris Associates

Analysis

Adjusted Income and Expense
YE 1/31

Year	2003	2002	2001
Revenue	370,394	296,303	224,389
% Change from prior year	25%	32%	
Cost of Sales:			
Beginning Inventories			
Purchases	96,719	89,124	64,912
Labor	87,446	68,600	40,285
less Ending Inventories			
Cost of Sales Total	184,165	157,724	105,197
Gross Profit	186,229	138,579	119,192
Total Expenses	131,085	93,355	58,098
Income Before Taxes	**55,144**	**45,224**	**61,094**
Adjustments:			
Officer's Compensation			
Depreciation	13,782	21,985	4,488
Amortization	660	660	
Interest	1,198	527	37
Professional Fees	20,000	6,000	
Total Adjustments	35,640	29,172	4,525
Net Expenses	95,445	64,183	53,573
Discretionary Earnings *	**90,784**	**74,396**	**65,619**
Adjusted EBIT **	58,284	41,896	33,119
EBITD ***	38,284	35,896	33,119
EBIT ****	23,842	13,251	28,631

* Dollars available for new owner's compensation, acquisition debt service, actual depreciation reserves and return on
    invested capital.
** Adjusted EBIT = Earnings Before Interest, Taxes plus Depreciation and Adjustments (less an Appropriate Owner/Manager salary)
*** Earnings B4 Interest, Taxes and Depreciation
**** Earnings B4 Interest and Taxes

Other Information

What would you have to pay a person to manage/operate this business?

Yearly salary/wage	25,000
Health/life insurance	4,000
Federal/state employment taxes	3,500
Vehicle	-
Other	-
Total Cost of Manager	$ 32,500

How much should be spent annually to keep the facility and equipment in suitable condition to remain competitive? $ 5,000

Adjusted Balance Sheet

This exhibit estimates the Fair Market Value of Company assets and liabilities and separates those items included in a sale from those typically retained by management.

Assets	FMV Transferable Assets	FMV Retained Assets
Cash	12,500	12,500
Accounts receivable	0	
Inventory	30,000	
Equipment	10,000	
Vehicles	35,000	
Office equipment	5,000	
FMV of Transferable Assets	92,500	
FMV Value of Retained Assets		12,500

Cost to Replace

Purchasers routinely estimated the costs of creating a similar enterprise when considering the purchase of an existing business. This exhibit estimates the results of such an exercise.

	Estimated Cost to Replace
Inventories	35,000
Prepaid Expenses	1,500
Leasehold Improvements	3,500
Equipment and Machinery	10,000
Vehicles	45,000
Office Equipment	5,000
Organizational Expenses	1,000
Other	
Estimated Cost to Replace	**$ 101,000**

Estimated Liquidation Value

This exhibit calculates liquidation values of Company assets. Lenders routinely use this value when calculating collateral values for lending purposes.

	Fair Market Value	Liquidation Factor	Liquidation Value
Cash			
Accounts receivable			
Inventory	30,000	0.70	21,000
Equipment	10,000	0.50	5,000
Vehicles	35,000	0.95	33,250
Office equipment	5,000	0.40	2,000
Estimated Liquidation Value			**61,250**

Collateral Value of Transferable Assets

	Liquidation Value	Usual % Loan to Value	Collateral Value	
Cash		0.00	-	*
Accounts receivable		0.80	-	
Inventory	21000	0.50	10,500	*
Equipment	5000	0.70	3,500	
Vehicles	33250	0.80	26,600	
Office equipment	2000	0.90	1,800	
		0.50	-	
		0.80	-	
Estimated Collateral Value			$ **42,400**	

* Assets being retained, not part of sale

Bankability Analysis

The availability of financing and the ability to borrow have a significant impact on value. This exhibit measures the probability of obtaining third party financing.

Profitability   **Score**
  0 - History of losses, not yet profitable
  3 - Profitable with erratic prior earnings or
      profitable with new management   **4.5**
  6 - Very profitable with strong management team in place

Collateral
  0 - Outdated equipment/facility or minimal fixed assets
  3 - Serviceable equipment - readily sold   **4.0**
  6 - Substantial assets easily converted to cash

Operating Ratios
  0 - All operating ratios below industry norms
  3 - Most operating ratios at or better than industry norms   **4.0**
  6 - All operating ratios better than industry norms

Debt Capacity
  0 - Company burdened with substantial debt
  3 - Moderate debt   **1.5**
  6 - Company is debt free

Management
  0 - Start up with no prior experience in this business
  3 - Established business with experienced management or,
      Purchase with seller providing transition assistance or,   **3.0**
      Purchase of a recognized franchise
  6 - Established business, management to remain

Industry
  0 - Declining industry or an industry with a high failure rate
  3 - Stable industry, history of consistent profits,
      expectations of moderate growth   **4.0**
  6 - Dynamic and profitable industry, future growth and
      profitability assured

Environmental
  0 - Produces or uses a highly hazardous material(s)
  3 - Moderate but controllable amounts of material
      representing possible environmental risk   **6.0**
  6 - No process or material(s) representing environmental
      risk present

Record Keeping
  0 - Minimal records prepared by management
  3 - Financial statements prepared by respected CPA   **3.0**
      or accountant
  4 - Audited statements prepared by major accounting firm

                                          Company Score   **3.8**

Definition of Score
  0 to 2.5 Financing unlikely
  2.6 to 3.5 Limited financing possible
  3.6 to 4.5 Financing probable

Risk Analysis

This exhibit converts the probable subjective view of the Risk, Stability and other factors into a numeral that should represent an appropriate Capitalization Rate (Risk/Reward Ratio) for the business. It must be noted that a low rating (Zero or One) may prevent a sale from occurring unless the buyer is able to perceive the low rating as opportunity.

	Rating
Risk Rating	
0 - Continuity of income at risk	
3 - Steady income likely	**4.5**
6 - Growing income assured	
Competitive Rating	
0 - Highly competitive in an unstable market	
3 - Normal competitive conditions	**3.0**
6 - Few competitors, high cost of entry for new competition	
Industry Rating	
0 - Declining industry	
3 - Industry growing slightly faster than inflation	**4.0**
6 - Dynamic industry, rapid growth expected	
Company Rating	
0 - Recent start up, not established	
3 - Well established with satisfactory environment	**4.0**
6 - Long record of sound operation with outstanding reputation	
Company Growth Rating	
0 - Revenues have been declining	
3 - Steady growth slightly faster than inflation	**4.5**
6 - Dynamic growth rate	
Desirability Factor	
0 - No status, rough or dirty work	
3 - Respected business in a satisfactory environment	**5.0**
6 - Challenging business in an attractive environment	
Operating Ratios	
0 - All operating ratios well below industry norms	
3 - Most operating ratios at or slightly better than industry norms	**4.0**
6 - All operating ratios well above industry norms	
Liquidity Ratios	
0 - Company consistently burdened with heavy debt	
3 - Liquidity ratios at or slightly better than industry norms	**1.5**
6 - Low debt and Liquidity ratios above industry norms	

Capacity Rating
0 - Immediate and substantial expense required for growth
3 - Moderate growth possible without additional capital investment   **4.0**
6 - Rapid growth possible without capital infusion

Management Depth Rating
0 - Owner operated without supervisory depth
3 - Owner operated with some supervisory depth   **2.0**
6 - Management strata for smooth succession in place

Customer Base Rating
0 - Highly dependent upon one or few customers or sales segment
3 - Revenues evenly distributed   **4.5**
6 - No change in any one customer or sector will effect earnings

Marketability Rating
0 - Marginal or negative earnings, cash price demanded
3 - Initial investment commensurate with earnings, moderate growth possible   **3.0**
6 - Substantial cash flow, transaction readily financed,
    exciting opportunity for growth

Bankabilty Rating
0 - Banks or other lenders unwilling to fund transfer or growth
3 - Limited financing available   **3.0**
6 - Substantial funding available at competitive rates

Environmental Rating
0 - Produces or uses a large amount of hazardous materials, strict licensing
3 - Minimal amounts of hazardous materials used, no licensing required   **6.0**
6 - No hazardous materials used or produced

Union Rating
0 - Union shop
3 - No union, some unionization in the industry   **3.0**
6 - No union, no history of unions in the industry

Occupancy Rating
0 - No lease available, business is location sensitive
3 - Lease, with options, extends for eight years - rents predetermined   **3.0**
6 - Real estate included or long lease (15 years +) with predetermined rents

Total of Ratings	**59.0**
Divide by the number of ratings	**17.0**
Produces a Multiple of	**3.5**
or a Capitalization Rate of	**28.8%**

GENERAL CAPITALIZATION RATES

The rate of capitalization ("Cap Rate"), also known as the risk reward ratio, is commonly used in valuing businesses by the more sophisticated investor. As noted below, capitalization rates vary depending upon the business venture's risk as perceived by the buyer.

RISK	CAP RATE
High Risk	
Venture capital	60 - 100%
Start-up companies	50 - 60%
Medium High Risk	
Existing company,	
Mature products, company,	
and industry,	
Owner leaving,	
Easy market entry	35 - 50%
Medium Low Risk	
Established company,	
Existing markets,	
Normal competition,	
Owner may remain,	
Some ease of market entry	20 - 35%
Low Risk	
Established company,	
Established market,	
Little or no competition,	
Profitable, low-risk markets,	
Owner to remain,	
Difficult entry into market	10 - 20%
Risk Free	
Money Market Rate	3 - 10%

Value
and
The Marketplace

VALUATION

Introduction

A business is defined as an organized method of routinely producing revenues over a period of time; and fair market value, as stated by the Internal Revenue Service in Revenue Ruling 59-60, is "the price at which property would change hands between a willing buyer and a willing seller when the former is not under compulsion to buy and the latter is not under compulsion to sell; both parties having reasonable knowledge of relevant facts".

The worth of a business can be divided into two major categories:
1. The asset value - machinery, equipment, building, land, usable stock, and other legal rights.

2. The business/goodwill value - the premium, over asset value, which a buyer will pay for organization, historically recorded cash flows, and projected future earnings.

Factors which play a part in determining a business' value include:
· Market value of assets
· The value of rights, privileges, and knowledge.
· Historic trends, along with future projections of revenues, expenses, and cash flows.
· The perception of risk associated with the quality and continuity of earnings.
· The type or class of buyer that can be attracted to the opportunity and their perception of the opportunity represented.
· Aesthetic appeal.

The techniques and formulas which will be used in arriving at values, are those which are generally accepted by business buyers and their professional advisors.

Results assume buyer and seller are considering alternative investments, so that a transaction occurs when the economic incentive to purchase is equal to the economic incentive to sell.

Generally, there is no economic incentive to invest monies in a business which is not capable of producing a net income in excess of both an operator's salary, and a reasonable return on invested capital.

The application of financial formulas is generally straightforward. However, it must be recognized that the marketplace is made up of many buyers, and that each can make an estimate of value which may be generous or conservative, depending upon perceptions of a range of criteria.

Allowing for these differences is not always straightforward, since feeling, desires, and judgments must be quantified. Such considerations result in calculations which must take probability into account.

And so, a proper valuation will develop a range of values which indicates how the marketplace of the different buyers and investors is likely to view the business. This range suggests the highest price a seller can expect, and the lowest price a seller should accept.

Value

It must be clearly understood that, in all cases, values discussed do not presume any buyer assumption of The Company's debt, liabilities, and obligations which might exist at the time of a sale. All such items must be acknowledged as the responsibility of the ownership. It should be mentioned, however, that with proper planning, some items of debt and liability can be addressed as a part of the acquisition process.

In this same regard, it must be clear that the value of certain assets will flow directly to management from the company, rather than from the acquiror. These will presumably include company vehicles, cash and accounts receivable.

Methods and Techniques

There is a wide array of methods and techniques which can be utilized to value a business. Among those considered and not applied, were:
- Capitalization of Profits
- Rothschild Banking Formula
- Multiples of Revenue
- Rules of Thumb
- Comparison with Public Company Transactions

The approaches selected were deemed appropriate because of the history, size, and profile of the Company, and the segments of the marketplace that might participate in its purchase.

These approaches acknowledge asset value; but, more importantly, focus upon adjusted cash flows, excess earnings, return on investment, and capacity to carry debt.

THE MARKETPLACE

The current marketplace for companies is made up, essentially, of four types of acquirers. An outline description of each is as follows:

The Strategic Acquirer
- typically a large firm, usually a Public Company
- accustomed to long term planning
- economic considerations are evaluated; however, reason for acquisition is not always purely economic
- acquisition prompted by factors such as establishing new markets

The Corporate or Sophisticated Acquirer
- typically comes from a large company background
- employs "schooled" approach when determining value
- usually a high net worth individual, a group of individuals, an investor group, or a small corporation
- focuses on current and future, rather than past
- places primary emphasis on capitalization of earnings, and on the ability to finance and leverage a purchase

The Financial or Lifestyle Buyer
- usually an individual
- primary focus on income replacement and the opportunity to build equity
- major emphasis placed on historic and current conditions
- case for case, the perception of risk is likely to be higher than that of the strategic or corporate style acquirer

The Industry Buyer
- usually from within the same, or affiliated, field as the company
- primary focus is on a business' fixed assets
- presumes that the company will bring virtually all other value to the enterprise

The following sections address value from the varying perspectives of these buyers

Industry
or
Asset Buyer
Methods

Book Value Methods
(Transferable Assets)

Industry and other asset focused buyers predictably will perform an analysis of the value of transferable assets. This exhibit estimates the result of such an exercise.

	Book Value	Book Value Adjusted to FMV	Liquidation Value
Inventory		30,000	21,000
Equipment		10,000	5,000
Vehicles		35,000	33,250
Office equipment		5,000	2,000
		-	

Adjusted Book Value	**$**	**80,000**	
Liquidation Value			**$** **61,250**

Summary

Methods	Values	Weight	Extension
Book Value	-	0.00	-
Adjusted Book Value	80,000	0.90	72,000
Liquidation Value	61,250	0.10	6,125
	141,250	1.00	78,125

Straight Average	70,625		
Weighted Average		78,125	
Probable Industry Buyer Value		**$**	**75,000**

Financial
Buyer
Methods

Income Calculations

(Financial Buyer)

Buyers and their advisors will review historic financial performance in an effort to obtain a leve
comfort as to probable earnings levels available to them for: a salary for the new owner, acquisit
service and, replacement reserves. This exhibit displays the computations most often employed
purpose and estimates results of the exercise.

	Discretionary Earnings	Weight	Extension
2003	90,784	5	453,920
2002	74,396	4	297,584
2001	65,619	3	196,857
	-	0	-
	-	0	-
Totals	230,799	12	948,361

Most recent year	90,784	
Straight Average	76,933	
Weighted Average		79,030

Estimate of earnings that a Financial Buyer will perceive as available for acquisition	**$**	**90,000**

Basic Method

This method combines the two major elements of business value to calculate worth. The first method adds perceived earnings and assets at current market value. The second formula is essentially the same but considers the Barrier of Entry and uses up to two years of Discretionary Earnings to address the time required to start a business and bring it to a similar cash position. Two years is generally the maximum time period buyers will be willing to use.

First Method

Fair Market Value of Assets		92,500
plus		
One year Discretionary Earnings		90,000
Resultant Value		**182,500**

Second Method

Fair Market Value of Assets		92,500
plus		
Monthly Earning	7,500	
multiplied by # months to reach		
same level of profitability	24	180,000
Resultant Value		**272,500**

Average both methods to obtain Basic Value

Basic Method Value	**$**	**227,500**

Discretionary Earnings Method

This method addresses the three prime considerations of a Financial or Lifestyle Buyer :
1) Transaction financing, 2) a salary or wage and, 3) a return on invested capital. Discretionary Earnings are reduced for debt service and an appropriate return on investment or cost of capital. The result produces an amount approximating the down payment, typically 1/3 of the purchase price.

Discretionary Earnings		$	90,000
less 25% reserved for debt service	X		0.75
Buyer's expected wage or earnings			67,500
less Return on Investment (ROI) 10%		-	6,750
Buyer's net cash advantage			60,750
Divide by typical down payment of 33% =		=	184,091

Resultant Discretionary Earnings Value $ **184,091**

Comparable Sales Method

The sale price and down payment ratios are derived by combining sales data from several hundred completed transactions. These ratios are then applied to the subject company to derive estimated values.

Sale Price Ratios	Ratios	Down Payment Ratios	Ratios
Sale Price/Revenues	0.35	Down Pay/Revenues	0.15
Sale Price/Disc. Earnings	2.37	Down Pay/Disc. Earnings	1.02
Sale Price/Asset Value (FMV)	1.64	Down Pay/Asset Value (FMV)	0.71

Subject Business:		
Revenues	$	296,303
Discretionary Earnings		90,000
FMV Assets		92,500

Ratios applied to subject business

Sale Price	Weight	Extension	Down Payment	Weight	Extension
SP/Revenues	0	-	DP/Revenues	0	-
SP/Disc. Earnings	2	426,600	DP/Disc. Earnings	2	183,600
SP/Asset Value (FMV)	1	151,700	DP/Asset Value (FMV)	1	65,675
Totals	3	578,300		3	249,275

Probable Down Payment $ 83,092

Probable Sale Price $ 192,767

Cost to Replace

Most Financial Buyers will balance a sale price against their perception of the cost to create a similar business from scratch.

Inventories	35,000
Prepaid Expenses	1,500
Leasehold Improvements	3,500
Equipment and Machinery	10,000
Vehicles	45,000
Office Equipment	5,000
Organizational Expenses	1,000
Other	-

Estimated Cost to Replace Value   **$**   **101,000**

Debt Capacity Method

Discretionary Earnings are reduced by deducting: an appropriate owner/manager salary and actual depreciation reserves to determine earnings available for Debt Service. The value produced represents the level of debt this business could service given the current level of earnings.

Discretionary Earnings	$	90,000
less Owner/Manager Salary		32,500
less Depreciation/Replacement Reserves		5,000
Dollars available for Debt Service		52,500

Assumptions:

Interest Rate		9.0%
Term of Note (yrs)		5
Monthly Payment	$	4,375

Probable Debt Capacity Value   **$210,759**

Summary of Financial Buyer Values

This exhibit arrays the results produced by the various methods likely to be employed by the Financial buyer and weights them as to probability of use producing a summary value.

Methods	Values	Weight	Extension
Basic	227,500	0.25	56,875
Discretionary Earnings	184,091	0.25	46,023
Comparable Sales	192,767	0.25	48,192
Cost to Replace	101,000	0.10	10,100
Debt Capacity	210,759	0.15	31,614
	815,116	1.00	192,803

Straight Average Value	203,779

Weighted Average Value	192,803

Target Value	**$ 195,000**

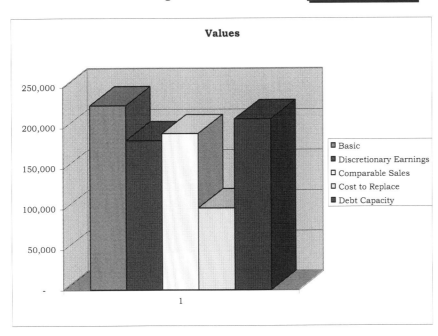

Convert Fair Market Value
to Fair Cash Value

Fair Market Value (FMV) is universally defined and generally accepted as a price received in "cash or equivalent." However, because financing for the acquisition of small and mid size businesses is restricted, the American Society of Appraisers (ASA) has redefined FMV for business transfers as "the price received under terms usual in the marketplace" i.e. Seller Financing. This exhibit measures the impact of restrictive financing and demands for a cash transaction and converts the Financial Buyer's terms price to Fair Cash Value.

Target Purchase Price	$	195,000
Usual Down Payment		70,000
Probable Bank Loan		42,000
Possible Cash at Transfer		112,000
Usual Seller's Note		83,000
Total Price (FMV)		195,000

1) Unfinanced portion of Transaction	42.6%
2) Divide by 2, add result to CAP rate as	
an adder for lack of financing	21.3%
3) CAP Rate for this business	28.8%
4) Discount Rate	50.1%

5) Apply Discount Rate to usual Seller's Note to calculate Present Value

	Annual note payments:	Present Value Factor	Present Value of Payments
1st year	21,895	0.666242	14,587
2nd year	21,895	0.443878	9,719
3rd year	21,895	0.295730	6,475
4th year	21,895	0.197028	4,314
5th year	21,895	0.131268	2,874

6) Present Value of usual Seller's Note	37,969
7) Add Cash at Transfer	112,000
Estimated Fair Cash Value	**149,969**

Justification of Purchase and Transaction Structure
(Financial Buyer)

Financial and Lifestyle Buyers generally expect the ratio of living wage to down payment to range between 70% and 90%. When the ratio drops below 70% our database of actual sales indicates that a transaction is unlikely to occur.

Example: The Financial Buyer with a down payment of $100K will typically expect a living wage of between $70K and $90K be available after debt service and replacement reserves.

Assumptions:	Seller's Note	Bank Note
Interest Rate	10.0%	10.0%
# Years Note	5.0	5.0
# Years Covenant not to Compete	5.0	
# Years Consulting Agreement	5.0	
The Ratios under this scenario equal:	**73.3%**	**60.0%**

Possible Structure:	Terms	Cash
Target Purchase Price	195,000	149,969
Down Payment	70,000	149,969
Covenant not to Compete	10,000	
Consulting Agreement	10,000	
Bank Note	42,000	
Seller's Note	63,000	
Total Purchase Price	195,000	

Annual Debt Service:		
Covenant not to Compete	2,000	
Consulting Agreement	2,000	
Bank Note	11,079	
Seller's Note	16,619	
Total Debt Service	31,699	

Discretionary Earnings	90,000	90,000
less Debt Service	(31,699)	
less Return on Buyer's on Cash Down	(7,000)	
Earnings available for Owner's Compensation and Depreciation reserves	$ 51,301	$ 90,000

Excess Earnings Method

This method blends the values of assets and earnings to determine the value of a business. A portion of Adjusted EBIT is assigned as a return on money invested in company assets. The remained is defined as Excess Earnings and is regarded as having been generated by the company's intangible assets - mainly goodwill. These Excess Earnings are then capitalized and added to the FMV of assets being acquired to produce a total value for all the tangible and intangible components of the business.

Adjusted EBIT		$ 60,000
Fair Market Value of Transferable Assets	80,000	
Times investment rate	15.0%	
Equals return on investment in company assets		12,000
Excess earnings		48,000
Capitalize excess earnings @		28.8%
Produces a value for the company's intangible assets		166,588
Plus FMV of assets being transferred		80,000
Resultant Value		**$ 246,588**

Discounted Present Profits

This method projects present earnings over a period of time and then calculates the present value of these earnings. The sum of the discounted earnings represents the present value of the expected future earnings. Present earnings are adjusted at a nominal rate to account for inflation.

Year	Adjusted EBIT	PV Factor 28.8%	Present Value of Earnings	Inflation Rate
1	60,000	0.776316	46,579	2.0%
2	61,200	0.602666	36,883	
3	62,424	0.467859	29,206	
4	63,672	0.363207	23,126	
5	64,946	0.281963	18,312	

Discounted Future Earnings Value $ **154,106**

Discounted Projected Earnings

This method, sometimes referred to as "Present Value of Future Earnings," uses projected earnings for a period of time and then calculates the present value of these earnings. The sum of the discounted earnings represents the present value of the expected future earnings.

End Year	Adjusted EBIT	Present Value Factor 28.8%	Present Value of Earnings
1	97,347	0.776316	75,572
2	119,629	0.602666	72,096
3	145,028	0.467859	67,853
4	173,882	0.363207	63,155
5	209,104	0.281963	58,959

Discounted Projected Earnings Value $ **337,636**

Multiple of EBIT Methods

EBIT methods are widely used and misused by many Sophisticated Buyers. EBIT and EBITD methods maybe inappropriate for many small and mid size companies as a significant amount of earnings generally have been recorded as discretionary expenses.

	Type EBIT		Range of Multiple	Range of Value		
			2	116,568		
1)	Adjusted EBIT	58,284	3	174,852		
			4	233,136		
	Appropriate Multiple		3			
	Probable Adjusted EBIT Value				$	174,852
2)	EBITD		3	114,852		
		38,284	4	153,136		
			5	191,420		
	Appropriate Multiple		4			
	Probable EBITD Value				$	153,136
3)	EBIT		4	95,368		
		23,842	5	119,210		
			6	143,052		
			7	166,894		
	Appropriate Multiple		6			
	Probable EBIT Value				$	143,052

Summary of EBIT Values:		Weight	
EBIT-DA	174,852	4	699,408
EBITD	153,136	2	306,272
EBIT	143,052	1	143,052
	471,040	7.00	1,148,732

Straight Average	157,013	
Weighted Average		164,105

Probable EBIT Method Value	$	160,000

Capitalization of Income

	Earnings	Cap Rate	Value	Wgt	Extension
Method #1 Capitalize most recent year's earnings	58,284	28.8%	202,280	0.20	40,456
Method #2 Capitalize average earnings	44,433	28.8%	154,209	0.10	15,421
Method #3 Capitalize weighted average earnings	50,966	28.8%	176,881	0.10	17,688
Method #4 Capitalize estimated current year	97,347	28.8%	337,853	0.30	101,356
Method #5 Capitalize historic & projected earnings	70,605	28.8%	245,042	0.05	12,252
Method #6 Capitalize estimated earnings	60,000	28.8%	208,235	0.25	52,059
			1,324,500	1.00	239,232
		Straight average	220,750		
		Weighted average			239,232

Probable Capitalization of Income Value $ 230,000

Summary of Sophisticated Buyer Methods

This exhibit summarizes and weights the various methods as to the probability of use thereby deriving a summary value.

Method	Value	Weight	Extension
Excess Earnings	246,588	0.30	73,976
Discounted Present Earnings	154,106	0.05	7,705
Discounted Projected Earnings	337,636	0.05	16,882
Capitalization of Earnings	230,000	0.30	69,000
Multiple of EBIT	160,000	0.30	48,000
	1,128,330	1.00	215,564
Straight Average Value	225,666		
Weighted Average Value	215,564		
Target Value		**$**	**220,000**

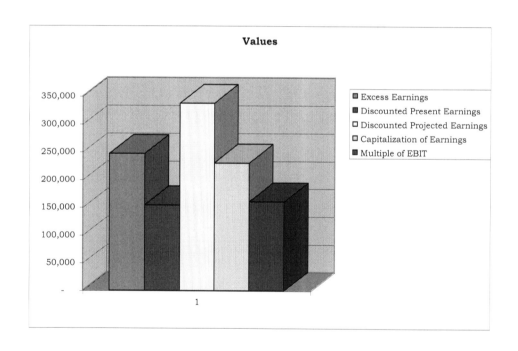

Convert Fair Market Value
to Fair Cash Value

Fair Market Value (FMV) is universally defined as a price received in "cash or equivalent." However, because financing for the acquisition of small and mid size businesses is restricted, the American Society of Appraisers (ASA) has redefined FMV for business transfers as "the price received under terms usual in the marketplace" i.e. Seller Financing. This exhibit measures the impact of restrictive financing and demands for a cash transaction and converts the Sophisticated Buyer's terms price to Fair Cash Value. It must be noted that the down payment typically is limited to $300,00 or less if the buyer is an individual.

Target Purchase Price	$	220,000
Usual Down Payment		75,000
Probable Bank Loan		42,000
Possible Cash at Transfer		117,000
Usual Seller's Note		103,000
Total Price (FMV)		220,000

1) Unfinanced portion of Transaction	46.8%
2) Divide by 2, add result to CAP rate as an adder for lack of financing	23.4%
3) CAP Rate for this business	28.8%
4) Discount Rate	52.2%

5) Apply Discount Rate to usual Seller's Note to calculate Present Value

Annual note payments:		Present Value Factor	Present Value of Payments
1st year	27,171	0.656932	17,850
2nd year	27,171	0.431560	11,726
3rd year	27,171	0.283506	7,703
4th year	27,171	0.186244	5,060
5th year	27,171	0.122350	3,324
6) Present Value of usual Seller's Note			45,664
7) Add Cash at Transfer			117,000

Estimated Fair Cash Value $ **162,664**

Summary of All Values

Industry or Asset Buyer Methods	Values	Weight		Extension
Book Value	-	-		-
Adjusted Book Value	80,000	0.90		72,000
Liquidation Value	61,250	0.10		6,125
		1.00		
Probable Industry Buyer Value			$	**75,000**

Financial or Lifestyle Buyer Methods	Values	Weight		Extension
Basic	227,500	0.25		56,875
Discretionary Earnings	184,091	0.25		46,023
Comparable Sales	192,767	0.25		48,192
Cost to Replace	101,000	0.10		10,100
Debt Capacity	210,759	0.15		31,614
		1.00		
Probable Financial Buyer Value			$	**195,000**
Estimated Cash Value	$ **149,969**			

Sophisticated or Corporate Buyer Methods	Values	Weight		Extension
Excess Earnings	246,588	0.30		73,976
Discounted Present Earnings	154,106	0.05		7,705
Discounted Projected Earnings	337,636	0.05		16,882
Capitalization of Earnings	230,000	0.30		69,000
Multiple of EBIT Methods	160,000	0.30		48,000
		1.00		
Probable Sophisticated Buyer Value			$	**220,000**
Estimated Cash Value	$ **162,664**			
Target Value			$	**220,000**

Conclusion

Buyer Identification

Of the four acquirer types, the first or Strategic Acquirer, is not a consideration as the Company lacks: proprietary processes, technologies or products to add synergy, or enter markets. Additionally, the Company's relative smallness (revenues under $20 million) would not meet the typical Strategic Acquirers minimum size requirements.

The Industry buyer is often confused with the Strategic Acquirer. Industry buyers lack strategic or synergistic motivations for purchase. Unlike Strategic Acquirers who focus on future benefits of technologies and market share, Industry Buyers generally focus only upon selected assets and resist acknowledging a company's intangible value or "Goodwill." In most situations this buyer is buyer of last resort. Exception to this rule occurs when:
*   company earnings are not commensurate with invested capital or,
*   operational skills are not readily transferable and firm lacks infrastructure for
    continuation without present owner

Corporate or Sophisticated Buyers are often the buyer of choice as they regularly take future earnings into account when assessing value. However, to attract this buyer prospects for future growth and profitability must be documented with credible and supportable assumptions.

The Financial buyer could find the Company attractive however; this buyer would need significant training and assistance from existing management as part of the purchase price. Additionally, this buyer's perception of risk would have a limiting effect on initial capital investments and heighten requests for significant levels of seller financing.

The sale of Client Company, Inc. would represent a marketing challenge for the following reasons:
*   Highly dependent upon present owner
*   Complex business
*   Company lacks management infrastructure that would remain after sale

Our perception, after reviewing all aspects of this business, is that it would most likely be acquired by a person displaying the characteristics of a Sophisticated Buyer. This buyer should be willing to pay $220,000 under terms as outlined in this report, or $162,000 in a cash transaction.

Sample Report

The retainer for this type of report typically ranges between $5,000 and $15,000

Marketplace Position and Summary of Values

Produced especially for

Client Company

Prepared by:
TTTTTT, FCBI
LLLLLLLL, LLC.
Telephone XXX.794-1200
Facsimile XXX.794-1042

Table of Contents

INTRODUCTION

This report has been prepared to accompany the presentation of Your Firm's work to date on behalf of Client Company, Inc. and is submitted to the company's ownership for review and approval in preparation for possible sale of the company. The Report is based on data and information provided by management. Results and conclusions can be no more accurate than this data and information allow.

This presentation, and accompanying data, are to be used as tools to:
- provide a marketplace view of this company
- understand this company's uniqueness, and the opportunity it represents
- identify the means for positioning the company so as to obtain the highest and best
- value
- develop an effective marketing plan built around the company's uniqueness
- determine what specific steps should be taken to further prepare the business for sale

The Report is organized to cover essential information regarding the following major areas of concern:

The Business and its Environment - a review of the company operations and competitive environment

A Business Analysis - an investigation of balance sheet, income statement, operating data, and industry information; so as to quantify the elements most likely to be considered when determining worth. These include values of tangible assets, historic and projected earnings and cash flows, and perception or risk.

The Marketplace and Valuations - definitions of value, an overview of the current marketplace for privately held businesses, an identification of probable kinds of acquirers for this business, a discussion of the techniques and approaches most likely to be used by the marketplace in establishing worth, and a summary of the values which result from the application of this thinking.

Transaction Structuring and Plan - a determination of the kinds of acquirers to be targeted, and the highest value they are likely to perceive. Discussion will also include an indication of the supporting data which is to be gathered and prepared as part of the marketing effort. Lastly, strategy and planning should identify probable elements of the sale transaction - elements such as non-compete agreements, down payment and the role of financing.

It must be clear that the validity of all of the information referenced above is limited in time. Market conditions and input data can cause conclusions and values to change. The duration over which this kind of information is valid depends heavily upon this business, its industry, and general economic conditions. Timely documentation of input data provides the means for determining whatever change might have taken place.

This report has been developed solely for Client Company and will not be presented to Investors.

For tax or legal advice, we encourage you to consult your accountant and/or attorney. Such advice must be based on the your individual situation and, therefore, be given by a qualified professional.

DATA SOURCES

All information describing the company has been obtained through interviews with the firm's owners, and from the company's books, records, and accountant's statements. Data regarding the industry, marketplace, and economy within which the company operates, has been obtained from:

- Annual Statement Studies - Robert Morris Associates
- US Department of Commerce
- Internal Revenue Service
- XXXXXX Department of Commerce
- YYYYYY Secretary of State

The Business
and its
Environment

The Company

XZXZXZ,Inc. (XZ) is an S Corporation whose president is its only shareholder. XZ was founded in 19XX in AAAAAA, BB as an authorized distributor of CCCCCC 2-Way Radio Equipment, and provides sales, repair service and rental, as well as system design and consultative services.

Products Provided and Serviced

XZ product lines include portable and mobile 2-way radios, base stations, repeaters, as well as rentals, batteries, parts and accessories, and it offers in house and on site repair and installation services.

Markets Served

Government entities, fire and safety, private/public sector security, mobile fleets, construction companies, warehousing, hospitality industry, property management all are prime candidates for XZ's products and services.

Two-way radios are used in a variety of applications including:

- Coordination of efforts between teams, departments and organizations
- Maintenance, construction and other wide ranging activities
- Public safety, emergency response and disaster relief
- Enhancement to existing communications
- SpeXZal events, promotions

Location

XZ moved from AAAAAA, BB to larger quarters at its present 2,200 square foot SSSSSSS, BB location in July 2000. This is a leased location near the intersection of Interstate 495 in an office/industrial park. The current lease is assignable and has options to renew to June 30, 2008 at predetermined rents.

Staff

XZ's staff consists of four non-family employees in addition to the president. All employees, past and present, have signed a non-compete agreement with XZ.

Position	Salary	Tenure	Benefits
Office Manager	$44,200	4 years	HMO, Vested SEP/IRA
Technical Sales Rep	34,320	5 years	HMO, Vested SEP/IRA, Car
TechniXZan	29,120	1 year	HMO
Service Manager	40,000	since 2/03	HMO

Benefits

Aetna HMO Health Insurance average cost is approximately $250 per employee per month.

Owner's Background

The President was a sales representative for MMMMM 2-way communication equipment for five years prior to founding XZ. He currently spends approximately five hours a week on sales and marketing with the balance of his time spent equally between Administrative duties and Personnel/FinanXZal management, and currently works 30-35 hours per week.

Operations

XZ operates five days a week from 8:30 A.M. to 5 P.M. Most sales and service activity is generated by incoming telephone calls. The source of the calls can be segregated as follows:

- Existing customers   50%
- Yellow Page advertising   20%
- Internet   20%
- Company Newsletter   10%

Sales/Marketing

As noted above XZ does not have an outside sales force. Most sales activity is in reaction to incoming calls from existing customers and advertising efforts. XZ mails 750 newsletters per quarter to customers and prospective customers. The Company also fax broadcasts announcements of speXZal promotions and sales to its existing customer base.

The Internet web site www.Communication3.com is generating an increasing amount of activity with an estimate of 4,000 visitors a month.

Segmentation of Sales

Details of sales and target gross profit by segment:

Segment	Estimate Volume	Target Gross Profit
2-way equipment sales	1,000,000	40%
2-way repairs	125,000	75%
2-way rentals	40,000	90%

Customer Concentrations

The top ten customers by percentage of sales

Year	2002	2001	2000
	17.9	7.8	6.9
	12.1	6.5	4.9
	4.5	4.7	4.6
	3.3	3.8	3.4
	2.4	2.8	3.0
	2.3	2.7	2.9
	2.3	2.2	2.5
	2.0	2.0	2.4
	1.7	1.9	2.2
	1.5	1.9	2.1
	50.0	63.7	64.9

> The top two customers in 2002 were Police and Federal government entities underlining the large opportunity that Homeland Security spending represents for the Company

Customers by Industry

Year	2002	2001	2000
	Police	School	Construction
	Federal	Construction	PA
	School	Retailer	Business Services
	Construction	Business Services	Property Management
	PA	Government	Hospitality
	College	Hospitality	Property Management
	Construction	Property Management	School
	Business Services	Contractor	Contractor
	Contractor	School	Contractor
	School	Janitorial	Property Management

The Industry

Several factors have combined to enhance the outlook for the 2-way communications industry:

- Increased security concerns and

- Government spending on Homeland Security

    2-way systems are not subject to congestion shutdowns such as those experienced during 9-11 by Nextel and other cellular telephones. In view of this, Federal, State and local governments as well as private sector entities are updating their communications equipment as part of their disaster preparedness planning.

- New FCC rules mandate equipment upgrades

The FCC has mandated upgrades of equipment capable of operating in "Narrow Band" frequenXZes (See Exhibit 1). It is these frequenXZes within which 2-way radios operate. Most existing equipment will therefore have to be replaced with equipment that conforms to the new rules.

Financial

Year	2002	2001	2000
Revenue	1,233,466	1,089,269	1,108,687
Cost of Sales Total	723,395	591,104	610,708
Gross Profit	511,071	498,165	497,979
Net Expenses	298,183	283,505	299,335
Discretionary Earnings*	212,888	214,660	198,644

* Dollars available for new owner's compensation, acquisition debt service, actual depreciation reserves and return on invested capital

XZ is a well-run company as the ratio analysis data in the Exhibit section of this report illustrates.

- Exhibit 2 - Comparative Operating Ratios

- Exhibit 3 - Ratios to Measure Safety and Liquidity

- Exhibit 4 - Ratios Measuring Operating Efficiency

Acquisition Financing

Pre-approvals for financing of amounts to $1,000,000 (including working capital) have been obtained and are in place. The candidate must have prior sales and management experience to qualify for this funding.

Assets

Assets to be included in the sale include all inventory, furniture, equipment, telephone numbers, goodwill, trademarks, trade names and other intangible assets.

Advantages this Business Represents

- Operates five days, Monday thru Friday 8:30 to 5:00, leaving weekends and evenings free for the rest of one's life

- The Two-way radio business enjoys healthy profit margins

- Increased security concerns elevate the need for XZ's products and services

- FCC has mandated replacement of existing 2-way radio systems over the next several years

- XZ represents the premier supplier in the industry

- XZ enjoys an excellent reputation for its technical abilities and customer service resulting in a loyal customer base that generates an above average amount of repeat business and referrals

Marketplace Economy

If employment rates are an indicator of economy trends, the economy in the marketplace served by XZ appears to be strong. Unemployment rates for the region are declining and are lower than the national average. Currently the national unemployment rate is 5.6 while XX and YY stand at 3.8 and 4.3 respectively.

Source: U. S. Bureau of Labor Statistics

State and Local Government Spending

Homeland Security Funding is becoming available. XZ's products and services will be needed by Schools, Hospitals, Universities, Police and Fire Departments and others. Below are the NIGP Code and Description of Products listed on the Commonwealth of Virginia's web-site.

NIGP Code	Description
72500	Radio Communication, Telephone, And Telecommunication Equipment, Accessories, And Supplies
72595	Recycled Communications Equipment (Including Batteries, Radios, Telephones, Telecommunication Equipment, etc.)

Opportunity

Develop an outside sales force to capitalize on the unique opportunities available for growth in sales and profits, i.e.:

- New FCC rules mandate equipment upgrades
- Increased security concerns
- Government spending on Homeland Security

Register as a vendor with XXXXXXX and YYYYYYY's cities, Counties, Schools, Hospitals, Fire and Police. The city of AAAAAAAA alone reports spending $400 million a year with registered vendors.

For information on becoming a registered Vendor in XXXXXX go to:

http://vendor shelp.dgs.state.XXX.us

YYYYYY's Procurement Web sites:
http://www.emarketplace.com/

http://comp/procurement.com

Opportunity (continued)

Add synergistic product lines to maximize the potential of existing capabilities of XZ, i.e.:

- Nextel and other cellular telephones

- In house paging systems

- CCTV and other security related systems

- Security related products such as police and fire light bars, sirens, bull horns, etc.

- AVL/GPS tracking systems

- Citizen band and other amateur radios

Industry Information Resources:

FCC Website http://www.fcc.gov/
Proposed Rules http://hraunfoss.fcc.gov/edocs_public/attachmatch/FCC-03-34A1.doc

American Mobile Telecommunication Association http://www.amtausa.org/

Canadian Wireless Telecommunication Association http://www.cwta.ca/

Federal Communications Commission (FCC) regulations

In 1995, the Federal Communications Commission (FCC) adopted regulations that will ultimately split each existing radio channel into four channels.

The rules adopted by the FCC envisioned that most people would transition to the 12.5 kHz bandwidth channels from the current 25 kHz bandwidth channels, and later transition to the 6.25 kHz bandwidth channels, as such equipment became available.

> Rather than requiring licensees and new applicants to meet the narrower bandwidth channeling by specific target dates, the FCC decided to encourage the transition to narrowband operations by requiring that new radio equipment submitted to the FCC for certification on or after February 14, 1997 must be capable of operation within a bandwidth of 12.5 kHz, and equipment submitted for certification on or after January 1, 2005 must be capable of operation with a bandwidth of 6.25 kHz.

However, the FCC allowed previously certificated 25 kHz bandwidth equipment to be sold indefinitely, allowing existing licensees of wideband equipment to continue purchasing such equipment to expand their radio systems and to license new systems.

The FCC reasoned that market forces would drive the transition to narrowband operations when it was in the interest of licensees to do so. As channels became increasingly congested or interference increased, licensees would have the incentive to buy more spectrally efficient, i.e. narrowband, equipment. The FCC believed that licensees operating in or near the major metropolitan areas would have the incentive to convert to narrow band equipment sooner because interference in those areas was greater, while licensees operating in remote areas, may be able to delay the conversion to narrow band for many years.

In 1998, the American Mobile Telecommunications Association (AMTA) filed a petition with the FCC stating that the transition to narrow band equipment was proceeding too slowly and asking the FCC to establish specific dates by which licensees would have to start using narrow band equipment or lose their primary status. The FCC has agreed that the conversion to narrow band equipment is proceeding too slowly, and has asked the public to comment on whether a mandatory transition date is necessary, and if so, what those dates should be.

FCC Releases Second Report and Order (R&O) and Second Further Notice of Proposed Rule Making (FNPRM)

Decisions made mandating the transition to narrowband technologies in the VHF and UHF Re-farming bands include:

1) Beginning six months after publication of this 2nd R&O in the Federal Register, prohibit any applications for new operations using 25kHz channels, for any system operating in the 150-174mHz or 421-512mHz refarming bands.

2) Beginning six months after publication of this 2nd R&O in the Federal Register, prohibit incumbent 25kHz Part 90 licenses in the 150-174mHz and 421-512mHz bands from making modifications to their systems that expand their respective authorized interference contours as a result thereof.

3) Beginning January 1, 2005, prohibit the certification of any equipment capable of operating at one voice path per 25kHz of spectrum, i,e., multi-mode equipment that includes a 25kHz mode.

4) Beginning January 1, 2008, prohibit the manufacture and importation of any 25kHz equipment (including multi-mode equipment that can operate on a 25kHz bandwidth).

5) Beginning January 1, 2013, require non-public safety licensees using channels in these bands to deploy technology that achieves the equivalent of one voice path per 12.5kHz of spectrum.

6) Beginning January 1, 2018, require public safety licensees using channels in these bands to deploy technology that achieves the equivalent of one voice path per 12.5kHz of spectrum.

The 2nd FNPRM seeks comment on additional issues related to promoting spectrum efficiency in the private land mobile radio services (PLMRS). The 2nd FNPRM seeks comment on whether the equipment certification provision in the current rules is sufficient to promote migration to one voice path per 6.25kHz bandwidth, or equivalent technology, or whether migration to 6.25kHz bandwidth or equivalent technology should be mandatory.

These rules are certain to be challenged by the filing of Petitions for reconsideration. We recommend regular viewing of the FCC website for further updates.

Analysis

Comparative Balance Sheets

YE 1/31/2001

Assets

Year	2002	2001	2000
Current Assets:			
Cash	81,979	37,222	45,357
Marketable Securities			
Accounts Receivable	63,709	73,763	111,033
Inventories	51,016	59,423	48,950
Loan's to Shareholders			
Prepaid Expenses			
Total Current Assets	**196,704**	**170,408**	**205,340**
Fixed Assets			
Leasehold Improvements			
Equipment and Machinery	90,231	87,166	67,301
Vehicles			
Office Equipment			
less Accumulated Depreciation	(80,621)	(71,036)	(63,298)
Total Fixed Assets	**9,610**	**16,130**	**4,003**
Other Assets			
CSV Life Insurance	0	0	0
Annuities	0	0	0
Other	2575	2525	2575
Total Other Assets	2,575	2,525	2,575
Total Assets	**208,889**	**189,063**	**211,918**

Comparative Balance Sheets (Continued)

Liabilities

Year	2002	2001	2000
Current Liabilities			
Accounts Payable	25,597	13,395	43,288
Accrued Profit Sharing			
Accrued Taxes			
Current Portion LT Debt			
Line of Credit		2,160	4,078
Notes to Shareholders	13,389	16,299	29,879
Total Current Liabilities	**38,986**	**31,854**	**77,245**
Long Term Liabilities			
Notes payable - Banks			
Noted payable - Other			
Deferred Income Taxes			
Capital Leases			
Other			
Total Long Term Liabilities	-	-	-
Total Liabilities	**38,986**	**31,854**	**77,245**
Stockholder's Equity	**169,903**	**157,209**	**134,673**
Total Assets and Liabilities	**208,889**	**189,063**	**211,918**

Other Information

What would you have to pay a person to manage/operate this business?

Yearly salary/wage	60,000
Health/life insurance	3,000
Federal/state employment taxes	7,500
Vehicle	
Other	-
Total Cost of Manager	$ 70,500

How much should be spent annually to keep the facility and equipment in suitable condition to remain competitive?   5,000

Adjusted Income and Expense
YE 12/31

Year	2002	2001	2000
Revenue	1,233,466	1,089,269	1,108,687
Cost of Sales:			
Beginning Inventories	59,423	48,950	68,794
Purchases	713,988	601,577	590,864
Labor			
less Ending Inventories	(51,016)	(59,423)	(48,950)
Cost of Sales Total	722,395	591,104	610,708
Gross Profit	511,071	498,165	497,979
Total Expenses	443,365	422,217	425,609
Income Before Taxes	**67,706**	**75,948**	**72,370**
Adjustments:			
Officer's Compensation	120,000	120,000	100,000
Depreciation	6,502	1,601	4,428
Interest		1,911	5,126
SEP deposit	10,804	9,487	15,000
Insurance	3,885	2,424	1,720
Auto expense	2,157	1,505	
Contributions	1,834	1,784	
Total Adjustments	145,182	138,712	126,274
Net Expenses	298,183	283,505	299,335
Discretionary Earnings *	**212,888**	**214,660**	**198,644**
Adjusted EBIT **	142,388	144,160	128,144
EBITD ***	123,708	128,960	111,424
EBIT ****	117,206	127,359	106,996

*   Dollars available for new owner's compensation, acquisition debt service, actual depreciation reserves and return on

      invested capital.

**   Adjusted EBIT = Earnings Before Interest, Taxes plus Depreciation and Adjustments (less an Appropriate Owner/Manager salary)

***   Earnings B4 Interest, Taxes and Depreciation

****   Earnings B4 Interest and Taxes

Adjusted Balance Sheet

This exhibit estimates the Fair Market Value of Company assets and liabilities and separates those items included in a sale from those typically retained by management

Assets	Book Value	Adjustment	FMV Transferable Assets	FMV Retained Assets
Cash	81,979			81,979
Marketable Securities	-			-
Accounts Receivable	63,709			135,000
Inventories	51,016		43,000	
Prepaid Expenses	-			-
Leasehold Improvements	-	-	-	
Equipment and Machinery	90,231	1,711	91,942	
Vehicles	-	10,000	10,000	
Office Equipment	-		-	
Other	2,575	-		2,575

FMV of Transferable Assets			144,942	
FMV Value of Retained Assets				219,554

Liabilities	Book Value	Adjustment	Transferable Liabilities	Retained Liabilities
Accounts Payable	25,597			25,597
Accrued Profit Sharing	-			-
Accrued Taxes	-			-
Current Portion LT Debt	-			-
Line of Credit	-			-
Notes to Shareholders	13,389			13,389
Notes payable - Banks	-			-
Noted payable - Other	-			-
Deferred Income Taxes	-			-
Capital Leases	-			-
Other	-			-
Book Value of Liabilities	38,986			
Value of Transferable Liabilities			-	
Value of Retained Liabilities				38,986

Residual Value		**180,568**

Cost to Replace

Purchasers routinely estimated the costs of creating a similar enterprise when considering the purchase of an existing business. This exhibit estimates the results of such an exercise.

	Book Value	Estimated Cost to Replace
Inventories	51,016	50,000
Prepaid Expenses	-	0
Leasehold Improvements	-	
Equipment and Machinery	90,231	100,000
Vehicles	-	25,000
Office Equipment	-	10,000
Organizational Expenses	-	500
Other	-	
Estimated Cost to Replace	**$**	**185,500**

Estimated Liquidation Value

This exhibit calculates liquidation values of Company assets. Lenders routinely use this when calculating collateral values for lending purposes.

	Fair Market Value	Liquidation Factor	Liquidation Value
Cash	81,979	1.00	81,979
Marketable Securities	-	1.00	-
Accounts Receivable	135,000	0.95	128,250
Inventories	43,000	0.85	36,550
Prepaid Expenses	-	0.90	-
Leasehold Improvements	-	-	-
Equipment and Machinery	91,942	0.70	64,359
Vehicles	10,000	0.90	9,000
Office Equipment	-	0.25	-
Other	2,575	0.50	1,288
Estimated Liquidation Value			**321,426**

Collateral Value of Transferable Assets

	Liquidation Value	Usual % Loan to Value	Collateral Value	
Accounts Receivable	128,250	0.00	-	*
Inventories	36,550	0.80	29,240	
Prepaid Expenses	-	0.00	-	*
Leasehold Improvements	-	0.70	-	
Equipment and Machinery	64,359	0.80	51,488	
Vehicles	9,000	0.90	8,100	
Office Equipment	-	0.50	-	
Other	1,288	0.80	1,030	
Estimated Collateral Value			$ 89,858	

* Assets being retained, not part of sale

Bankability Analysis

The availability of financing and the ability to borrow have a significant impact on value. This exhibit measures the probability of obtaining third party financing.

	Score
Profitability	
0 - History of losses, not yet profitable	
3 - Profitable with erratic prior earnings or	
profitable with new management	**5.0**
6 - Very profitable with strong management team in place	
Collateral	
0 - Outdated equipment/facility or minimal fixed assets	
3 - Serviceable equipment - readily sold	**3.0**
6 - Substantial assets easily converted to cash	
Operating Ratios	
0 - All operating ratios below industry norms	
3 - Most operating ratios at or better than industry norms	**4.0**
6 - All operating ratios better than industry norms	
Debt Capacity	
0 - Company burdened with substantial debt	
3 - Moderate debt	**5.5**
6 - Company is debt free	
Management	
0 - Start up with no prior experience in this business	
3 - Established business with experienced management or,	
Purchase with seller providing transition assistance or,	**4.5**
Purchase of a recognized franchise	
6 - Established business, management to remain	
Industry	
0 - Declining industry or an industry with a high failure rate	
3 - Stable industry, history of consistent profits,	
expectations of moderate growth	**4.0**
6 - Dynamic and profitable industry, future growth and	
profitability assured	
Environmental	
0 - Produces or uses a highly hazardous material(s)	
3 - Moderate but controllable amounts of material	
representing possible environmental risk	**5.5**
6 - No process or material(s) representing environmental	
risk present	
Record Keeping	
0 - Minimal records prepared by management	
3 - Financial statements prepared by respected CPA	**4.0**
or accountant	
4 - Audited statements prepared by major accounting firm	
Company Score	**4.4**

Definition of Score

0 to 2.5 Financing unlikely
2.6 to 3.5 Limited financing possible
3.6 to 4.5 Financing probable

Risk Analysis

This exhibit converts the probable subjective view of the Risk, Stability and other factors into a numeral that should represent an appropriate Capitalization Rate (Risk/Reward Ratio) for the business. It must be noted that a low rating (Zero or One) may prevent a sale from occurring unless the buyer is able to perceive the low rating as opportunity.

Risk Rating	**Rating**
0 - Continuity of income at risk	
3 - Steady income likely	**4.0**
6 - Growing income assured	

Competitive Rating	
0 - Highly competitive in an unstable market	
3 - Normal competitive conditions	**3.0**
6 - Few competitors, high cost of entry for new competition	

Industry Rating	
0 - Declining industry	
3 - Industry growing slightly faster than inflation	**4.0**
6 - Dynamic industry, rapid growth expected	

Company Rating	
0 - Recent start up, not established	
3 - Well established with satisfactory environment	**4.5**
6 - Long record of sound operation with outstanding reputation	

Company Growth Rating	
0 - Revenues have been declining	
3 - Steady growth slightly faster than inflation	**2.5**
6 - Dynamic growth rate	

Desirability Factor	
0 - No status, rough or dirty work	
3 - Respected business in a satisfactory environment	**5.0**
6 - Challenging business in an attractive environment	

Operating Ratios	
0 - All operating ratios well below industry norms	
3 - Most operating ratios at or slightly better than industry norms	**4.0**
6 - All operating ratios well above industry norms	

Liquidity Ratios
0 - Company consistently burdened with heavy debt
3 - Liquidity ratios at or slightly better than industry norms   **5.5**
6 - Low debt and Liquidity ratios above industry norms

Capacity Rating
0 - Immediate and substantial expense required for growth
3 - Moderate growth possible without additional capital investment   **4.5**
6 - Rapid growth possible without capital infusion

Management Depth Rating
0 - Owner operated without supervisory depth
3 - Owner operated with some supervisory depth   **4.0**
6 - Management strata for smooth succession in place

Customer Base Rating
0 - Highly dependent upon one or few customers or sales segment
3 - Revenues evenly distributed   **3.0**
6 - No change in any one customer or sector will effect earnings

Marketability Rating
0 - Marginal or negative earnings, cash price demanded
3 - Initial investment commensurate with earnings, moderate growth possible   **4.5**
6 - Substantial cash flow, transaction readily financed,
     exciting opportunity for growth

Bankabilty Rating
0 - Banks or other lenders unwilling to fund transfer or growth
3 - Limited financing available   **4.5**
6 - Substantial funding available at competitive rates

Environmental Rating
0 - Produces or uses a large amount of hazardous materials, strict licensing
3 - Minimal amounts of hazardous materials used, no licensing required   **5.5**
6 - No hazardous materials used or produced

Union Rating
0 - Union shop
3 - No union, some unionization in the industry   **3.0**
6 - No union, no history of unions in the industry

Occupancy Rating
0 - No lease available, business is location sensitive
3 - Lease, with options, extends for eight years - rents predetermined   **3.0**
6 - Real estate included or long lease (15 years +) with predetermined rents

Total of Ratings	**64.5**
Divide by the number of ratings	**17.0**
Produces a Multiple of	**3.8**
or a Capitalization Rate of	**26.4%**

GENERAL CAPITALIZATION RATES

The rate of capitalization ("Cap Rate"), also known as the risk reward ratio, is commonly used in valuing businesses by the more sophisticated investor. As noted below, capitalization rates vary depending upon the business venture's risk as perceived by the buyer.

RISK	CAP RATE
High Risk	
Venture Capital	60 - 100%
Start-Up Companies	50 - 60%
Medium High Risk	
Existing Company,	
Mature Products,	
Company, Industry,	
Owner Leaving,	
Easy Market Entry	35 - 50%
Medium Low Risk	
Established Company,	
Existing Markets, Normal	
Competition, Owner May	
Remain, Somewhat Ease	
of Market Entry	20 - 35%
Low Risk	
Established Company,	
Established Market,	
Little or No Competition,	
Profitable, Low-Risk	
Markets, Owner Remain,	
Difficult Entry into Market	10 - 20%
Risk Free	
Money Market Rate	3 - 10%

Value
and
The Marketplace

VALUATION

Introduction

A business is defined as an organized method of routinely producing revenues over a period of time; and fair market value, as stated by the Internal Revenue Service in Revenue Ruling 59-60, is "the price at which property would change hands between a willing buyer and a willing seller when the former is not under compulsion to buy and the latter is not under compulsion to sell; both parties having reasonable knowledge of relevant facts".

The worth of a business can be divided into two major categories:
1. The asset value - machinery, equipment, building, land, usable stock, and other legal rights.

2. The business/goodwill value - the premium, over asset value, which a buyer will pay for organization, historically recorded cash flows, and projected future earnings.

Factors which play a part in determining a business' value include:
   · Market value of assets
   · The value of rights, privileges, and knowledge.
   · Historic trends, along with future projections of revenues, expenses, and cash flows.
   · The perception of risk associated with the quality and continuity of earnings.
   · The type or class of buyer that can be attracted to the opportunity and their perception of the opportunity represented.
   · Aesthetic appeal.

The techniques and formulas which will be used in arriving at values, are those which are generally accepted by business buyers and their professional advisors.

Results assume buyer and seller are considering alternative investments, so that a transaction occurs when the economic incentive to purchase is equal to the economic incentive to sell.

Generally, there is no economic incentive to invest monies in a business which is not capable of producing a net income in excess of both an operator's salary, and a reasonable return on invested capital.

The application of financial formulas is generally straightforward. However, it must be recognized that the marketplace is made up of many buyers, and that each can make an estimate of value which may be generous or conservative, depending upon perceptions of a range of criteria.

(Continued)

Introduction (continued)

Allowing for these differences is not always straightforward, since feeling, desires, and judgements must be quantified. Such considerations result in calculations which must take probability into account.

And so, a proper valuation will develop a range of values which indicates how the marketplace of the different buyers and investors is likely to view the business. This range suggests the highest price a seller can expect, and the lowest price a seller should accept.

Value

It must be clearly understood that, in all cases, values discussed do not presume any buyer assumption of The Company's debt, liabilities, and obligations which might exist at the time of a sale. All such items must be acknowledged as the responsibility of the ownership. It should be mentioned, however, that with proper planning, some items of debt and liability can be addressed as a part of the acquisition process.

In this same regard, it must be clear that the value of certain assets will flow directly to management from the company, rather than from the acquirer. These will presumably include company vehicles, cash and accounts receivable.

Methods and Techniques

There is a wide array of methods and techniques which can be utilized to value a business. Among those considered and not applied, were:
 · Capitalization of Profits
 · Rothschild Banking Formula
 · Multiples of Revenue
 · Rules of Thumb
 · Comparison with Public Company Transactions
The approaches selected were deemed appropriate because of the history, size, and profile of the Company, and the segments of the marketplace that might participate in its purchase.

These approaches acknowledge asset value; but, more importantly, focus upon adjusted cash flows, excess earnings, return on investment, and capacity to carry debt.

THE MARKETPLACE

The current marketplace for companies is made up, essentially, of four types of acquirers. An outline description of each is as follows:

The Strategic Acquirer
· typically a large firm, usually a Public Company
· accustomed to long term planning
· economic considerations are evaluated; however, reason for acquisition is not always purely economic.
· acquisition prompted by factors such as establishing new markets.

The Corporate or Sophisticated Acquirer
· typically comes from a large company background
· employs "schooled" approach when determining value
· usually a high net worth individual, a group of individuals, an investor group, or a small Corporation
· focuses on current and future, rather than past
· places primary emphasis on capitalization of earnings, and on the ability to finance and leverage a purchase.

The Financial or Lifestyle Buyer
· usually an individual
· primary focus on income replacement and the opportunity to build equity
· major emphasis placed on historic and current conditions.
· case for case, the perception of risk is likely to be higher than that of the strategic or corporate style acquirer.

The Industry Buyer
· usually from within the same, or affiliated, field as the company.
· primary focus is on a business' fixed assets.
· presumes that they will bring virtually all other value to the enterprise.

The following sections address value from the varying perspectives of these buyers.

Industry
or
Asset Buyer
Methods

Book Value Methods
(Transferable Assets)

Industry and other asset focused buyers predictably will perform an analysis of the value of transferable assets. This exhibit estimates the result of such an exercise.

	Book Value	Book Value Adjusted to FMV	Liquidation Value
Inventories	51,016	43,000	36,550
Equipment and Machinery	90,231	91,942	64,359
Vehicles	-	10,000	9,000
Office Equipment	-	-	-
Other	2,575	-	1,288
Less Depreciation	(80,621)		
Book Value	**$ 63,201**		
Adjusted Book Value		**$ 144,942**	
Liquidation Value			**$ 111,197**

Methods	Values	*Summary* Weight	Extension
Book Value	63,201	0.10	6,320
Adjusted Book Value	144,942	0.80	115,954
Liquidation Value	111,197	0.10	11,120
	319,340	1.00	133,393

Straight Average	106,447		
Weighted Average		133,393	
Probable Industry Buyer Value		$	**145,000**

Financial
Buyer
Methods

Income Calculations
(Financial Buyer)

Buyers and their advisors will review historic financial performance in an effort to obtain a level of comfort as to probable earnings levels available to them for: a salary for the new owner, acquisition debt service and, replacement reserves. This exhibit displays the computations most often employed for this purpose and estimates results of the exercise.

	Discretionary Earnings	Weight	Extension
2002	212,888	5	1,064,440
2001	214,660	4	858,640
2000	198,644	3	595,932
1999	-	0	-
1998	-	0	-
Totals	626,192	12	2,519,012

Most recent year   212,888

Straight Average   208,731

Weighted Average   209,918

Estimate of earnings that a Financial Buyer will perceive as available for acquisition $ 213,000

Basic Method

This method combines the two major elements of business value to calculate worth. The first method adds perceived earnings and assets at current market value. The second formula is essentially the same but considers the Barrier of Entry and uses up to two years of Discretionary Earnings to address the time required to start a business and bring it to a similar cash position. Two years is generally the maximum time period buyers will be willing to use.

First Method

Fair Market Value of Assets		144,942
plus		
One year Discretionary Earnings		213,000
Resultant Value		**357,942**

Second Method

Fair Market Value of Assets		144,942
plus		
Monthly Earning	17,750	
multiplied by # months to reach		
same level of profitability	24	426,000
Resultant Value		**570,942**

Average both methods to obtain Basic Value

Basic Method Value	$	**464,442**

Discretionary Earnings Method

This method addresses the three prime considerations of a Financial or Lifestyle Buyer :
1) Transaction financing, 2) a salary or wage and, 3) a return on invested capital. Discretionary Earnings are reduced for debt service and an appropriate return on investment or cost of capital. The result produces an amount approximating the down payment, typically 1/3 of the purchase price.

Discretionary Earnings	$	213,000
less 25% reserved for debt service	X	0.75
Buyer's expected wage or earnings		159,750
less Return on Investment (ROI) 10%	-	15,975
Buyer's net cash advantage		143,775
Divide by typical down payment of 33% =	=	435,682

Resultant Discretionary Earnings Value $ **435,682**

Cost to Replace

Most Financial Buyers will balance a sale price against their perception of the cost to create a similar business from scratch.

Inventories	50,000
Prepaid Expenses	0
Leasehold Improvements	-
Equipment and Machinery	100,000
Vehicles	25,000
Office Equipment	10,000
Organizational Expenses	500
Other	-

Estimated Cost to Replace Value   **$ 185,500**

Debt Capacity Method

Discretionary Earnings are reduced by deducting: an appropriate owner/manager salary and actual depreciation reserves to determine earnings available for Debt Service. The value produced represents the level of debt this business could service given the current level of earnings.

Discretionary Earnings	$	213,000
less Owner/Manager Salary		70,500
less Depreciation/Replacement Reserves		-
Dollars available for Debt Service		142,500

Assumptions:

Interest Rate		9.0%
Term of Note (yrs)		5
Monthly Payment	$	11,875

Probable Debt Capacity Value   **$572,059**

Summary of Financial Buyer Values

This exhibit arrays the results produced by the various methods likely to be employed by the Financial buyer and weights them as to probability of use producing a summary value.

Methods	Values	Weight	Extension
Basic	464,442	0.25	116,111
Discretionary Earnings	435,682	0.30	130,705
Comparable Sales	415,775	0.30	124,732
Cost to Replace	185,500	-	-
Debt Capacity	572,059	0.15	85,809
	2,073,458	1.00	457,356

Straight Average Value	414,692	
Weighted Average Value	457,356	
Target Value	**$ 450,000**	

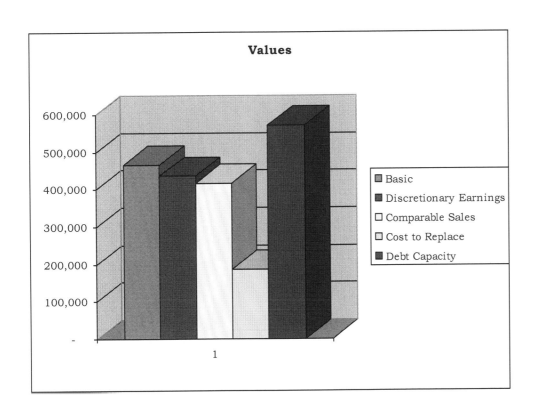

Convert Fair Market Value
to Fair Cash Value

Fair Market Value (FMV) is universally defined and generally accepted as a price received in "cash or equivalent." However, because financing for the acquisition of small and mid size businesses is restricted, the American Society of Appraisers (ASA) has redefined FMV for business transfers as "the price received under terms usual in the marketplace" i.e. Seller Financing. This exhibit measures the impact of restrictive financing and demands for a cash transaction and converts the Financial Buyer's terms price to Fair Cash Value.

Target Purchase Price	$	450,000
Usual Down Payment		179,143
Probable Bank Loan		90,000
Possible Cash at Transfer		269,143
Usual Seller's Note		180,857
Total Price (FMV)		450,000

1) Unfinanced portion of Transaction   40.2%
2) Divide by 2, add result to CAP rate as
    an adder for lack of financing   20.1%
3) CAP Rate for this business   26.4%
4) Discount Rate   46.5%
5) Apply Discount Rate to usual Seller's Note to calculate Present Value

	Annual note payments:	Present Value Factor	Present Value of Payments
1st year	47,710	0.682818	32,577
2nd year	47,710	0.466241	22,244
3rd year	47,710	0.318358	15,189
4th year	47,710	0.217381	10,371
5th year	47,710	0.148432	7,082

6) Present Value of usual Seller's Note   87,463
7) Add Cash at Transfer   269,143

Estimated Fair Cash Value   **356,606**

Justification of Purchase and Transaction Structure
(Financial Buyer)

Financial and Lifestyle Buyers generally expect the ratio of living wage to down payment to range between 70% and 90%. When the ratio drops below 70% our database of actual sales indicates that a transaction is unlikely to occur.

Example: The Financial Buyer with a down payment of $100K will typically expect a living wage of between $70K and $90K be available after debt service and replacement reserves.

Assumptions:	Seller's Note	Bank Note
Interest Rate	7.5%	7.5%
# Years Note	10.0	10.0
# Years Covenant not to Compete	5.0	
# Years Consulting Agreement	5.0	

The Ratios under this scenario equal:	**86.5%**

Possible Structure:	Terms
Target Purchase Price	450,000
Down Payment	180,000
Covenant not to Compete	
Consulting Agreement	
Bank Note	90,000
Seller's Note	180,000
Total Purchase Price	450,000

Annual Debt Service:	
Covenant not to Compete	-
Consulting Agreement	-
Bank Note	13,112
Seller's Note	26,223
Total Debt Service	39,335

Discretionary Earnings	213,000
less Debt Service	(39,335)
less Return on Buyer's on Cash Down	(18,000)
Earnings available for Owner's Compensation and Depreciation reserves	$ 155,665

Sophisticated or Corporate Buyer Methods

Comparative Operating Ratio Review

This exhibit reviews the operating history of the company. This information is often used to project future levels of profitability.

Year	2002	2001	2000
Sales	1,233,466	1,089,269	1,108,687
Cost of Sales	722,395	591,104	610,708
Ratio	58.6%	54.3%	55.1%
Period Average	56.1%		
Cost of Goods	722,395	591,104	610,708
Ratio	58.6%	54.3%	55.1%
Period Average	56.1%		
Labor Cost	-	-	-
Ratio	0.0%	0.0%	0.0%
Period Average	0.0%		
Net Expenses	298,183	283,505	299,335
Ratio	24.2%	26.0%	27.0%
Period Average	25.7%		
Income Before Taxes	**67,706**	**75,948**	**72,370**
Ratio	5.5%	7.0%	6.5%
Period Average	6.3%		
Discretionary. Earnings	**212,888**	**214,660**	**198,644**
Ratio	17.3%	19.7%	17.9%
Period Average	18.2%		
Adjusted EBIT	142,388	144,160	128,144
Ratio	11.5%	13.2%	11.6%
Period Average	8.0%		
EBIT	123,708	128,960	111,424
Ratio	10.0%	11.8%	10.1%
Period Average	6.5%		
Officer Compensation	120,000	120,000	100,000
Ratio	9.7%	11.0%	9.0%
Period Average	9.9%		

Comparative Ratio Analysis (Continued)

Ratios to Measure Return on Investment (ROI)

Return on Equity Measures the return on the investments made by the owners

Net Income	67,706	75,948	72,370
Stockholder's Equity	169,903	157,209	134,673
Ratio	40%	48%	54%

Return on Assets Measures return on investment in assets employed in the business.

Net Income	67,706	75,948	72,370
Total Assets	208,889	189,063	211,918
Ratio	32%	40%	34%

Ratios to measure Safety and Liquidity

Net Working Capital Measures ability to meet short term obligations.

Current Assets	196,704	170,408	205,340
- Current Liabilities	38,986	31,854	77,245
	157,718	138,554	128,095

Current Ratio Measusres ability to pay current liabilities as they mature. A ratio of 1:1 or greater equates to positive net working capital.

Current Assets	196,704	31,854	77,245
Current Liabilities	483,275	463,573	530,793
Ratio	0.8	0.9	1.3

Quick Ratio Also known as the "Acid Test" ratio, it is a refinement of the Current Ratio and is a more conservative measure of liquidity. The ratio expresses the degree to which a company's current liabilities arecovered by the most liquid current assets.

Cash, Accts & Notes Receivable	81,979	37,222	45,357
Total Current Liabilities	483,275	463,573	530,793
Ratio	0.17	0.08	0.09

Debt to Equity Calculates balance between total equity and long term debt. The larger the percentaage, the more the company is leveraged.

Long-term Debt	0	0	0
Stockholder's Equity	169,903	157,209	134,673
Ratio	0%	0%	0%

Debt Service Ratio Indicator of a firm's ability to pay both interest and principal on its outstanding debt.

Adjusted EBIT	142,388	144,160	128,144
Interest & principal paymts	14,689	11,911	16,720
Ratio	9.7	12.1	7.7

Sales/WorkingCapital Working capital is a measure of the margin of protection for current creditors. This ratio reflects the firm's ability to finance current operations

Net Sales	1,089,269	1,108,687	0
Net Working Capital	157,718	138,554	128,095
Ratio	6.9	8.0	0.0

Ratios Measuring Operating Efficiency

Collection Period Calculates number of days' sales that are uncollected in average accounts receivables. Provides insight as to effectiveness in collecting customer debts.

Accounts Receivable	63,709	73,763	111,033
Daily sales	2,984	3,037	0

Projections

This exhibit estimates profitability at various revenue levels. Investors and their advisors can be expected to perform this exercise as they review the viability of an investment or purchase.

	Projected Current Yr.	Case 1	Case 2	Case 3	Case 4	Case 5
Target Revenues	1,300,000	1,500,000	1,700,000	1,900,000	2,100,000	2,300,000
Target % Cost of Sales*	56.1%	56.1%	56.1%	56.1%	56.1%	56.1%
Target $ Cost of Sales	728,989	841,141	953,293	1,065,446	1,177,598	1,289,750
Gross Profit	571,011	658,859	746,707	834,554	922,402	1,010,250
Target Net Expenses	320,000	350,000	375,000	425,000	450,000	500,000
Discretionary Earnings	251,011	308,859	371,707	409,554	472,402	510,250
Adjusted EBIT	180,511	238,359	301,207	339,054	401,902	439,750
Target Ratios:						
Gross Profit	43.9%	43.9%	43.9%	43.9%	43.9%	43.9%
Net Expenses	24.6%	23.3%	22.1%	19.7%	20.2%	19.6%
Adjusted EBIT	13.9%	15.9%	17.7%	17.8%	19.1%	19.1%

* Period average used

Income Computations
(Sophisticated Buyer)

Buyers and their advisors will use various methods in determining the amount of earnings available for the transaction. A review of historic results and their perception of the opportunity will flavor their conclusions. Note that projections are taken into account and an Owner/Manager's wage is deducted from Discretionary Earnings (Adjusted EBIT).

Year	Adjusted EBIT	Wgt	Extension	Wgt	Extension
2007	401,902			1	401,902
2006	339,054			2	678,109
2005	301,207			3	903,620
2004	238,359			4	953,435
Est. Current Yr.	180,511	0	-	5	902,555
2002	142,388	5	711,940	5	711,940
2001	144,160	4	576,640	4	576,640
2000	128,144	3	384,432	3	384,432
1999	(70,500)	2	(141,000)	2	(141,000)
1998	(70,500)	1	(70,500)	1	(70,500)
	273,692	15	1,461,512	30	5,301,133

Most recent yr.	142,388

5 Year Straight average	54,738

Weighted average	97,434

Weighted historic and future average	176,704

Estimated Current Year	180,511

Estimated First Year	238,359

Estimate of earnings that a Sophisticated Buyer will perceive as available for acquisition $ **180,000**

Excess Earnings Method

This method blends the values of assets and earnings to determine the value of a business. A portion of Adjusted EBIT is assigned as a return on money invested in company assets. The remained is defined as Excess Earnings and is regarded as having been generated by the company's intangible assets - mainly goodwill. These Excess Earnings are then capitalized and added to the FMV of assets being acquired to produce a total value for all the tangible and intangible components of the business.

Adjusted EBIT		$ 180,000
Fair Market Value of Transferable Assets	144,942	
Times investment rate	15.0%	
Equals return on investment in company assets		21,741
Excess earnings		158,259
Capitalize excess earnings @		26.4%
Produces a value for the company's intangible assets		600,452
Plus FMV of assets being transferred		144,942
Resultant Value		**$ 745,394**

Discounted Present Profits

This method projects present earnings over a period of time and then calculates the present value of these earnings. The sum of the discounted earnings represents the present value of the expected future earnings. Present earnings are adjusted at a nominal rate to account for inflation.

Year	Adjusted EBIT	PV Factor 26.4%	Present Value of Earnings	Inflation Rate
1	180,000	0.791411	142,454	2.0%
2	183,600	0.626331	114,994	
3	187,272	0.495686	92,828	
4	191,017	0.392291	74,934	
5	194,838	0.310463	60,490	

Discounted Future Earnings Value $ 485,701

Discounted Projected Earnings

This method, sometimes referred to as "Present Value of Future Earnings," uses projected earnings for a period of time and then calculates the present value of these earnings. The sum of the discounted earnings represents the present value of the expected future earnings.

End Year	Adjusted EBIT	Present Value Factor 26.4%	Present Value of Earnings
1	238,359	0.791411	188,640
2	301,207	0.626331	188,655
3	339,054	0.495686	168,064
4	401,902	0.392291	157,663
5	439,750	0.310463	136,526
	Discounted Projected Earnings Value	$	**839,548**

Multiple of EBIT Methods

EBIT methods are widely used and misused by many Sophisticated Buyers. EBIT and EBITD methods maybe inappropriate for many small and mid size companies as a significant amount of earnings generally have been recorded as discretionary expenses.

	Type EBIT		Range of Multiple	Range of Value		
			2	284,776		
1)	Adjusted EBIT	142,388	3	427,164		
			4	569,552		
	Appropriate Multiple		**3.5**			
	Probable Adjusted EBIT Value				$	**498,358**
2)	EBITD		3	371,124		
		123,708	4	494,832		
			5	618,540		
	Appropriate Multiple		**4.5**			
	Probable EBITD Value				$	**556,686**
3)	EBIT		4	468,824		
		117,206	5	586,030		
			6	703,236		
			7	820,442		
	Appropriate Multiple		**5.5**			
	Probable EBIT Value				$	**644,633**

Summary of EBIT Values:		Weight		
EBIT-DA	498,358	4	1,993,432	
EBITD	556,686	2	1,113,372	
EBIT	644,633	1	644,633	
	1,699,677	7.00	3,751,437	
Straight Average	566,559			
	Weighted Average		535,920	

Probable EBIT Method Value $ **550,000**

Capitalization of Income

	Earnings	Cap Rate	Value	Wgt	Extension
Method #1 Capitalize most recent year's earnings	142,388	26.4%	540,237	0.20	108,047
Method #2 Capitalize average earnings	54,738	26.4%	207,684	0.10	20,768
Method #3 Capitalize weighted average earnings	97,434	26.4%	369,677	0.10	36,968
Method #4 Capitalize estimated current year	238,359	26.4%	904,361	0.30	271,308
Method #5 Capitalize historic & projected earnings	176,704	26.4%	670,437	0.05	33,522
Method #6 Capitalize estimated earnings	180,000	26.4%	682,941	0.25	170,735
			3,375,337	1.00	641,349
		Straight average	562,556		
		Weighted average			641,349

Probable Capitalization of Income Value $ 600,000

Summary of Sophisticated Buyer Methods

This exhibit summarizes and weights the various methods as to the probability of use thereby deriving a summary value.

Method	Value	Weight	Extension
Excess Earnings	745,394	0.50	372,697
Discounted Present Earnings	485,701	0.00	-
Discounted Projected Earnings	839,548	0.00	-
Capitalization of Earnings	600,000	0.30	180,000
Multiple of EBIT	550,000	0.20	110,000
	3,220,643	1.00	662,697

Straight Average Value	644,129
Weighted Average Value	662,697

Target Value   **$**   **700,000**

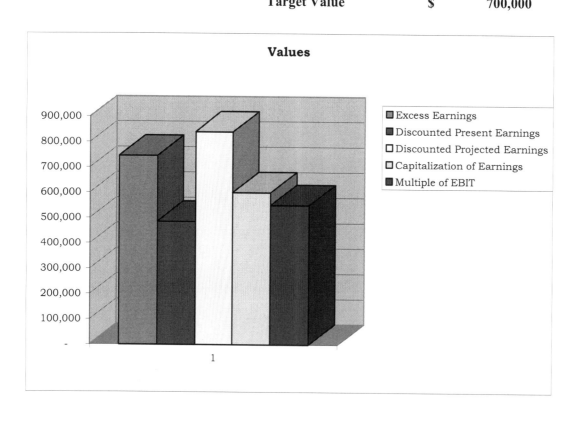

Convert Fair Market Value
to Fair Cash Value

Fair Market Value (FMV) is universally defined as a price received in "cash or equivalent." However, because financing for the acquisition of small and mid size businesses is restricted, the American Society of Appraisers (ASA) has redefined FMV for business transfers as "the price received under terms usual in the marketplace" i.e. Seller Financing. This exhibit measures the impact of restrictive financing and demands for a cash transaction and converts the Sophisticated Buyer's terms price to Fair Cash Value. It must be noted that the down payment typically is limited to $300,00 or less if the buyer is an individual.

Target Purchase Price	$	700,000
Usual Down Payment		100,000
Probable Bank Loan		600,000
Possible Cash at Transfer		700,000
Usual Seller's Note		-
Total Price (FMV)		700,000

1) Unfinanced portion of Transaction	0.0%
2) Divide by 2, add result to CAP rate as an adder for lack of financing	0.0%
3) CAP Rate for this business	26.4%
4) Discount Rate	26.4%
5) Apply Discount Rate to usual Seller's Note to calculate Present Value	

		Present Value Factor	Present Value of Payments
Annual note payments:			
1st year	-	0.791411	-
2nd year	-	0.626331	-
3rd year	-	0.495686	-
4th year	-	0.392291	-
5th year	-	0.310463	-
6) Present Value of usual Seller's Note			-
7) Add Cash at Transfer			700,000

Estimated Fair Cash Value	**$**	**700,000**

Justification of Purchase and Transaction Structure
(Sophisticated Buyer)

Corporate or Sophisticated Acquirers - will deduct an appropriate manager's salary, debt service and reserves for depreciation from Discretionary Earnings and then calculate the return on their initial investment (ROI). The ROI should approximate the capitalization rate developed as a measure of risk appropriate to the opportunity (plus or minus 10%).

Example: Discretionary Earnings of $350K less an appropriate owner/manager salary divided by the initial investment will produce an ROI percentage.

	$350K	Discretionary Earnings
less	250K	Salary, Debt service and Depreciation Reserves
equals	$100K	$ Return on Investment (ROI)
divided by	400K	Down Payment
equals	25%	% Return on Investment (ROI)

Assumptions:	Seller's Note	Bank Note
Interest Rate	7.5%	7.5%
# Years Note		10.0
# Years Covenant not to Compete	5.0	
# Years Consulting Agreement	5.0	

The Capitalization Rate developed for this company is:		26.4%
The Ratio under this scenario equal:	82.6%	
Possible Structure:	**Terms**	
Target Purchase Price	700,000	
Down Payment	100,000	
Bank Loan	600,000	
Covenant not to Compete	-	
Consulting Agreement	-	
Seller's Note	-	
Total Purchase Price	700,000	
Annual Debt Service:		
Covenant not to Compete	-	
Consulting Agreement	-	
Seller's Note		
Bank Note	87,412	
Total Debt Service	87,412	
Adjusted EBIT	180,000	
less Debt Service	(87,412)	
less Return on Buyer's on Cash Down	(10,000)	
Buyer's Return on invested capital	$ 82,588	

Summary
and
Conclusion

Summary of All Values

Industry or Asset Buyer Methods	Values	Weight	Extension
Book Value	63,201	0.10	6,320
Adjusted Book Value	144,942	0.80	115,954
Liquidation Value	111,197	0.10	11,120
		1.00	
Probable Industry Buyer Value			**$ 145,000**

Financial or Lifestyle Buyer Methods			
Basic	464,442	0.25	116,111
Discretionary Earnings	435,682	0.30	130,705
Comparable Sales	415,775	0.30	124,732
Cost to Replace	185,500	-	-
Debt Capacity	572,059	0.15	85,809
		1.00	
Probable Financial Buyer Value			**$ 450,000**
Estimated Cash Value	**$ 356,606**		

Sophisticated or Corporate Buyer Methods			
Excess Earnings	745,394	0.50	372,697
Discounted Present Earnings	485,701	-	-
Discounted Projected Earnings	839,548	-	-
Capitalization of Earnings	600,000	0.30	180,000
Multiple of EBIT Methods	550,000	0.20	110,000
		1.00	
Probable Sophisticated Buyer Value			**$ 700,000**
Estimated Cash Value	**$ 700,000**		
Target Value			**$ 700,000**

Conclusion

Buyer Identification

Of the four acquirer types, the first or Strategic acquirer, is not a consideration as the Company lacks: proprietary processes, technologies or products to add synergy, or enter markets. Additionally, the Company's relative smallness (revenues under $20 million) would not meet the typical Strategic acquirers minimum size requirements.

The Industry buyer is often confused with Strategic acquirers. Industry buyers lack strategic or synergistic motivations for purchase. Unlike Strategic acquirers who focus on future benefits of technologies and market share, Industry buyers generally focus only upon selected assets and resist acknowledging a company's intangible value or "Goodwill." In most situations this buyer is buyer of last resort. Exception to this rule occurs when:
* company earnings are not commensurate with invested capital or,
* operational skills are not readily transferable and firm lacks infrastructure for continuation with out present owner

Corporate or Sophisticated buyers are often the buyer of choice as they regularly take future earnings into account when assessing value. However, to attract this buyer prospects for future growth and profitability must be documented with credible and supportable assumptions.

The FinanXZal buyer could find the Company attractive however, this buyer would need significant training and assistance from existing management as part of the purchase price. Additionally, this buyer's perception of risk would have a limiting effect on initial capital investments and heighten requests for significant levels of seller finanXZng.

The sale of Client Company, Inc. would represent a considerable marketing challenge for the following reasons:
* Highly dependent upon present owner
* Complex business
* Company lacks management infrastructure that would remain after sale
* Consolidating industry

Our perception, after reviewing all aspects of this business, is that it would most likely be acquired by a person displaying characteristics of a Sophisticated buyer. This buyer should be willing to pay $700,000 in a cash transaction.

Sample Report #3

The fee collected for this report was $25,000

Created especially for

Sample Industries, Inc.

Marketplace Position and Summary of Values

Date

This document contains confidential and proprietary information. The analysis contained within this document was derived from many different sources of information. This document may contain forward-looking statements that may relate to analyses and other information that are based on estimates that are not yet determinable. These statements may contain risks and uncertainties about the future that may cause the Company's actual future activities and results of operations to be materially different than those suggested or described in this document. Readers of this document are cautioned to not place undue reliance on forward-looking statements. YOUR FIRM, INC. and its Agents or Affiliates, is not responsible for updating or revising any forward-looking statements, whether as a result of new information discovered or future events identified.

CONTENTS

Introduction

This report has been prepared to accompany the presentation of YOUR FIRM, INC'S work to date on behalf of Sample Corporation and is submitted to the Company's ownership for review and approval in preparation for a possible sale of the company. The Report is based on data and information provided by Management. Results and conclusions can be no more accurate than this data and information allow.

This presentation, and accompanying data, is to be used as tools to:
· Provide a marketplace view of this company
· Understand this company's uniqueness, and the opportunity it represents
· Identify the means for positioning the company so as to obtain the highest and best value
· Develop an effective marketing plan built around the company's uniqueness
· Determine what specific steps should be taken to further prepare the business for sale

The Report is organized to cover essential information regarding the following major areas of concern:
General Overview – an overview of the industry and its future outlook, general competition and trends identified, including, where appropriate, government regulations impacting the industry.

A Business Analysis - an investigation of balance sheet, income statement, operating data, and industry information; so as to quantify the elements most likely to be considered when determining worth. These include values of tangible assets, historic and projected earnings and cash flows, and perception of risk.

The Marketplace and Valuations - definitions of value, an overview of the current marketplace for privately held businesses, an identification of probable kinds of acquirers for this business, a discussion of the techniques and approaches most likely to be used by the marketplace in establishing worth and a summary of the values which result from the application of this thinking.

Transaction Structuring and Plan - a determination of the kinds of acquirers to be targeted and the highest value they are likely to perceive. Discussion will also include an indication of the supporting data that is to be gathered and prepared as part of the marketing effort. Lastly, strategy and planning should identify probable elements of the sale transaction - elements such as non-compete agreements, down payment and the role of financing.

It must be clear that the validity of all of the information referenced above is limited in time. Market conditions and input data can cause conclusions and values to change. The duration over which this kind of information is valid depends heavily upon this business, its industry, and general economic conditions. Timely documentation of input data provides the means for determining whatever change might have taken place. This report has been developed solely for Sample Corporation and will not be presented to Investors.

For tax or legal advice, we encourage you to consult your accountant and/or attorney. Such advice must be based on your individual situation and, therefore, be given by a qualified professional.

All information describing the company has been obtained through interviews with the firm's owners, and from the company's books, records and accountant's statements. Data regarding the industry, marketplace, and other relevant information within which the company operates, has been obtained from a number of sources (e.g. proprietary databases, trade journals, etc.).

Profile

Industry

Overview and Outlook

With over 1,900 fastener distributors nationwide, the Fastener industry has a good presence on the map. It represents approximately $7.8 billion in revenues. Each distributor has, on average, less than 5% of the market. 1,500 of the companies are privately held and generate sales of less than $2 million per year. Only 3 suppliers have sales that exceed $100 million per year. The following table reflects the general breakdown of companies in the industry. The Company falls in the $2-5 million range.

Sales Volume	# Co's (est.)	%
$100 Million+	3	0.1%
$50-100	10	0.5%
$25-50	11	0.6%
$10-25	60	3.1%
$5-10	110	5.6%
$2-5	270	13.8%
<$2 million	1,500	76.4%
Total	1,964	100.0%

The automotive, aerospace and construction industries demand the most from the industry. Fasteners are also heavily used in communications, machinery, small appliance and electrical components industries. Among all the different types of fasteners, externally threaded fasteners have historically represented about 40% of total fastener sales. There is no slow down predicted for this industry. It is expected to grow by 3-4% annually through 2008 to a $10.2 billion industry. The construction market is going to remain healthy for years to come. Automotive sales already went through their slump in the mid '90s and should rebound well. Telecommunications have had their issues, but the communications industry is not going away. Machinery always has to be maintained or repaired. The same goes for small appliances and electrical components. In short, the fastener industry is here to stay and will continue to grow.

If your business was solely supplying to the automotive industry, then your business was hit hard in 2001. The average automobile uses over $100 of fasteners. When automobile sales are down, that segment of the fastener industry suffers. During 2002 and the coming years, the automotive industry is expected to rebound, having a positive impact on the fastener industry.

Building material and supply stores sell more fasteners than any other outlet. Currently, sales in the building material and supply group exhibit the strongest growth and capture more of the market every year. In 1998, businesses in the building material and supply group represented 48.6 percent of total fastener sales compared to only a 25 percent share captured by hardware stores. If your business falls into the building materials and supply group, you are well positioned in the market.

Competition

Fasteners manufactured overseas offer some competition to the U.S. market. Foreign fastener manufacturers use a cheaper labor force than the U.S. and have supplied end users in the U.S. with inexpensive, low-grade materials for quite some time. American manufacturers of fasteners are focusing on more expensive, technical products. Customers are demanding more specific requests, requiring American manufacturers to produce more technical products. Foreign manufacturers are not producing the more technical products. As a result, American made, higher dollar, more technical products are showing a demand in the overseas markets.

For select applications, adhesives are considered a product substitute for fasteners. More times than not a traditional fastener will do the job better and last longer than an adhesive. There has been growth of adhesives and non-mechanical fasteners in the market, which poses competition for traditional fastener distributors who do not supply adhesives. The adhesive technology is improving year by year and may pose more of a threat to fastener distributors in the future.

Trends

Throughout the late 90's mergers were wide spread in the fastener industry. The companies that were strong survived. Larger end users were demanding lower distributed costs. Companies either merged or were acquired to reduce their overhead structures, increase their volumes and/or realize cost savings to

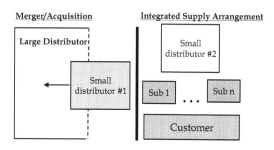

offer a lower priced product to compete more effectively on price. The larger end users sought to source products from a single supplier. Distributors developed integrated supply arrangements, providing many products (beyond what the company stores in its own warehouse) to a customer. The integrated supply arrangement allows a distributor to function as a general contractor. The general contractor selects subcontractors that provide complementary products and can provide the same quality and service levels to the general contractor's customer.

The larger distributors have always had more breadth of products to offer its customers. For those smaller distributors that established an integrated supply arrangement, they are better positioned in the market place. The subcontractors that are part of the consortium do act independent of one another, but those that work together well can compete effectively with the larger players.

In today's market, independent fastener distributors find that focusing on service is a key differentiator in the market. Those distributors that are part of a consortium must continue to turn around product quickly or else the large end user will bring its business elsewhere. Those that perform have created a one-stop shopping model for the larger end users. If a distributor has proven itself, a larger end user may allow the distributor to manage its inventory needs and the larger end user will rely on the performance of the distributor to ship products to it just in time.

Many distributors that have developed these integrated supply arrangements have typically done so on a smaller, more local scale and have not yet branched to the national or global level. Companies that can develop the systems/controls and can manage the breadth first will be a dominant force in the industry.

For most manufacturers and distributors, the manufacturer-distributor relationship has grown tighter over time. The mergers that have occurred in the industry over the last 5 years have made it more "complicated and binding." Many manufacturers have placed significant pressure on distributors to supply much if not all of the manufacturer's outsourced needs. Manufacturers have basically shifted the inventory management risk to the distributor. Many times the distributor has found it to be financially rewarding but sometimes it is a bit risky. The manufacturer has the customer loyalty. The customer depends on a particular fastener for its needs. The distributor ends up holding the inventory, hoping the customer remains active and loyal to the product.

To survive, independent fastener distributors must make every effort possible to offer the best service, reliability, availability, quality and depth of supply. They must ensure the accounts they serve have some sort of 'legal, binding commitment', to cover the risk of inventorying regular, and most often 'unique,' items. Such 'blanket orders' can tie up significant dollars and cause serious cash problems for the independent distributor when they are not honored.

Similar to ISO 9000, the Fastener Quality Act was established to ensure there was a degree of standardization and quality compliance in the industry. As a result, end users could better depend on the quality of the product being purchased. With the establishment of this Act, customers could further depend on the quality of the product, further supporting the future demand for the product.

During 1999, distributors and manufacturers received some relief from the original Act. The original Act posed additional burdens on the industry, requiring that all products be tested, regardless of lot size. In 1999, the Amendment exempted lots smaller than 75 units from testing (small lot exemption). There are concerns in the industry regarding this loophole and the government is seeking alternatives to manage this exemption process while not posing undue burdens on the industry.

Company

Overview

Sample Corporation has been a family run business for over 50 years. The company was founded in XXXX. It is a full line distributor of industrial products and provides a variety of services. The company not only distributes fasteners but also supplies abrasives, hand and power tools, paint, hydraulic and pneumatic hose, fittings, chains, cutting tools, safety equipment, material handling equipment, filters and much more. The company is an authorized GGGGG Company stocking distributor and has a hose fabrication shop inside its operations.

Its services range from fabricating hoses, customizing rods and building stockroom inventory programs to managing customers' inventory levels. Over a period of time, Sample has developed strong supplier alliances with other subcontractors (a.k.a. integrated supply arrangements), where Sample offers its customers a broader product line (beyond its existing inventory) with the same service level it offers to all of its customers.

The Company is based in West YYYYY, BB. Having been around for over 50 years, it has proven itself to be a strong competitor. In the industry, it is known to be among the top 20% of the players and directly competes with the Home Depots and Lowes of the world.

Sample started in the equipment hardware supply business during the construction of the YYYYYY Turnpike and since has serviced many large projects and businesses in the region such as; the MMMM Air Force Base, DDDD Nuclear Power, Edison Plants, SSSS Airport, early warning radar project in Alaska, Major project, 17 trash to energy plants and 4 coal to energy plants to name a few. The Company has over 1,000 active customers in Manufacturing, Construction, State and Local Government, Healthcare, and Bio-Technology.

Within the State and Local Government sector, Sample stands out above the rest. It has a strong reputation with the State of BB and has successfully locked in a statewide contract where many purchases for 5 major contracts flow directly through Sample.

Through its integrated supply arrangements it offers environmental products, material handling equipment, HVAC filters, automotive shop equipment, fasteners & tools, janitorial supplies and paints and wallpapers.

Environmental Products	Floor maintenance chemicals, restroom sanitary cleaners and food service papers and trash bags.
Material handling	Conveyors, lifts, safety / shop equipment, rack storage, casters and much more
HVAC Air filters	Air purifiers, air filters, air filtration systems and air cleaners for manufacturing, educational, commercial, scientific, technological and home use
Automotive shop equip	Vehicle maintenance facilities with all the major products
Fasteners & tools	A full range of fastener products, hydraulic & pneumatic hose and fittings and a complete line of hand tools and abrasives.
Janitorial supplies	Janitorial, maintenance, lubricants and ground products available throughout integrated supply network
Paints & wallpapers	Full line manufacturing and distribution of paints, industrial coatings, wall coverings, and window treatments.

Sample strongly supports the just-in-time manufacturing theory. With many of its customers, it has a vendor managed inventory program in place. On a periodic basis, Sample counts the inventory at a customer site and maintains the minimum/maximum levels designated in their customer's warehouse(s). The customer is able to optimize its inventory levels and reduce administrative burdens associated with purchasing.

Customers within the fastener industry expect a distributor to provide high service levels, provide one stop shopping, be flexible and agile with the customer, keep the inventory to a minimum, find ways to reduce the total cost of product/distribution while maintaining the quality imposed by the Fastener Quality Act. Sample does all of this and more.

With its strong customer relationships and their vendor managed inventory programs, Sample knows what the customer needs and can predict the inventory levels with a reasonable degree of certainty. They maintain a low overhead structure and therefore can pass on the lower costs to their customers posing heavy price competition for its competitors that have higher overhead costs.

With its own fleet of trucks, it is able to maintain its 24-hour turnaround time to service all of the region. Third party carriers are used to service customers beyond the region. The company has consistently quoted realistic time frames to its customers. As a result, customers know what to expect and know that Sample will be there when they say they will. That consistency and reliability has brought Sample to where it is today.

Operations

The company operates out of a 7,000 square foot facility servicing over 1,300 active customers on an annual basis. Having been in the same location for nearly 50 years, it has developed a presence for the local clientele for a walk-in service. The retail segment is small but provides additional cash flow to the business.

Company Profile

Years in Existence	50
Square Footage	7,000
# Active customers	1,300
# subcontractors	14
Entire customer base	Not solely dependent
State Business	40-50% of business
Top 50 customers	80% of business
Average customer	<1% of sales
30% of customers	>50% margins
40% of customers	> 25% margins

Sample has been quite astute in its integrated supply arrangements with 14 different subcontractors. The larger fastener distributors have always posed a serious threat to the smaller player. The larger distributors have the breadth to offer many products. Smaller ones have limited shelf space and have, in the past, only been able to offer what is in their warehouse. To compete, some smaller players (like Sample) have moved toward integrated supply arrangements, working closely with a consortium of subcontractors to supply many products to the customer. Even though they act independent of one another, these consortiums allow the smaller distributors to compete with the larger players. Sample finds that approximately 1/3rd of its revenues come from these arrangements.

The business does not rely on any one customer for the bulk of its sales; it is well distributed among its customers. The typical customer accounts for less than 1% of the business. With a well-established state contract, the business can rely on consistent and more predictable results from the state agencies. Given the recent economic times, state agencies accounted for 40-50% of the business enabling Sample to better weather the economic bumps. During the first half of 2002, Sample had approximately 425 customers. The top 50 customers accounted for 80% of the total sales. Approximately 30% of the customers provided over 50% gross margins to the business with an additional 40% providing a minimum of 25% gross margins. Sample also has approximately 239 vendors it does business with during the first half of 2002. Among these vendors, approximately 35 vendors represent the largest dollars purchased. See below for a summary table and further commentary.

The following summarizes a brief analysis performed on the 2001 revenue breakdown by customer and vendor breakdown that was provided for the 6 months ended June 30, 2002. Some figures have been estimated in the analyses.

Financial Results

The following summarizes the financial results over the past 3+ years. With the exception of 2002, the Company has shown growth year by year. Due to the current economic times, many companies have had a drop in sales upwards of 20%+. Sample has not faced as dramatic of a decline as other companies.

Financial Results

| | Thru 6/30 | | | |
	2002	**2001**	**2000**	**1999**
Revenue	2,432,272	5,378,112	4,576,142	3,195,680
Cost of Sales	1,545,125	4,283,215	3,572,272	2,220,815
Gross Profit	887,147	1,094,897	1,003,870	974,865
Net Expenses	375,531	765,628	688,961	656,277
Net Income	511,616	329,269	314,909	318,588

Customer Breakdown

Looking at the entire business, the top 10 customers represent approximately 35% of the business. State related business accounts for 48% of the business with the remainder covered by a variety of other customers.

With only 10 customers (excluding the state business) representing 35% of the entire business, a potential buyer might find the customer base not well diversified posing undue risk. If 1 of those customers chose to move its business to a competitor, revenues could drop between $50,000-100,000 impacting the overall profitability of the business.

When you include the state business, with the exception of the top 2 customers, no one customer exceeds 5%. From an entire business perspective, the customer base appears in good shape. Once the state business is removed, it is less so distributed.

Description	Revenue ($'s)	%
Top 10 customers (non-state related)	$960,000	35%
State related business	1,325,000	48%
Other	465,000	17%
Total (6 mos.)	$2,750,000	100%

Revenue Breakdown by Sales Person

Approximately 79% of the revenues are being generated and/or handled by XXXX. Based on this information, a buyer may perceive the business as being heavily dependent on XXXXX's relationships and knowledge that may impact the overall value of the business. A buyer would find that by having other people do more of the work, there would be less risk in the business.

Salesperson	Sales Volume	Percent
XXXXX	2,146,659	79%
YYYYY	253,111	9%
MMMM	257,575	10%
JJJJJJ	27,258	1%
SSSSSS	25,728	1%

Orders/Line Items by Sales Person

It appears that 57% of total orders/line items are handled directly by XXXXX. It would be assumed the business is highly dependent on XXXXX providing quotes and processing customer orders. A buyer would perceive that he/she would have to function in a similar role, limiting him/her from running other areas of the business, potentially impacting perceived value.

Salesperson	Sales Volume	Percent
XXXXX	10.467	57%
YYYYY	2,497	14%
MMMM	3,099	17%
JJJJJJ	878	5%
SSSSSS	1,359	7%

Margin % by Sales Person

With the assumption that each sales person does not solely focus on selling or servicing <u>one</u> product, it appears that people in the business price products differently. This can have a significant impact on the bottom line. For instance, by standardizing pricing that is processed through XXXX (say, an additional 3-4% to reach YYYYY's pricing), the business could be generating an additional $50-100,000 to the bottom line, increasing the overall value of the company. The $50-100,000 uses the assumption that XXX handles about 79% of the business noted above.

Salesperson	**ProfitPercent**
XXXXX	**27.3%**
YYYYY	**31.7%**
MMMM	**00.5%**
JJJJJJJ	**7.8%**
SSSSSS	**32.8%**

Vendor Analysis

Except for MMMM Co., PPPPPP and AA, no one vendor exceeds 5% of the total purchases for the 6 months ended June 30, 2002. This indicates the company is fairly well distributed among its supplier base. The company does fall into what is commonly referred to as the 80/20 rule; 80% of the purchases falls within 20% of the vendors being purchased from. In other words, of all of your purchases placed with your suppliers (total of 239 suppliers for the 6 mos. ended in June, 2002), only 35 vendors represent the highest dollars purchased. The administrative burdens the Company expends on all these small suppliers might not be worth it. You might be able to obtain some volume discounts and fewer administrative headaches by placing orders with other suppliers and consolidating your supplier base. You must be careful not to consolidate too much so you do not become too "dependent" on any one vendor.

Description	$	%	#
Larger purchased dollars	1,624,178	80	35
Lower purchased dollars	377,442	20	204
Totals	2,001,620	100	239

Financial Analysis

Comparative Balance Sheets

Below reflects the comparative balance sheet data to support figures used in the various valuation methods.

YE 12/31				
Assets	Thru 6/30			
Year	**2002**	**2001**	**2000**	**1999**
Current Assets:				
Cash	63,422	155,118	232,893	82,838
Marketable Securities			-	
Accounts Receivable	777,107	354,331	501,705	392,870
Inventories	67,642	60,000	40,000	32,100
Loan's to Shareholders				
Prepaid Expenses				
Total Current Assets	**908,171**	**569,449**	**774,598**	**507,808**
Fixed Assets				
Leasehold Improvements				
Equipment and Machinery		140,931	127,773	116,192
Vehicles				
Office Equipment				
less Accumulated Depreciation		(80,770)	(84,046)	(71,524)
Total Fixed Assets	**69,224**	**60,161**	**43,727**	**44,668**
Other Assets				
CSV Life Insurance	0	0	0	0
Annuities	0	0	0	0
Other	0	0	0	0
Total Other Assets				
Total Assets	**977,395**	**629,610**	**818,325**	**552,476**
Liabilities				
Current Liabilities				
Accounts Payable	90,654	277,157	88,951	79,939
Accrued Profit Sharing				
Accrued Taxes	2,044			
Current Portion LT Debt	84,750	181,000	182,685	181,185
Line of Credit				
Notes to Shareholders				
Total Current Liabilities	**177,448**	**458,157**	**271,636**	**261,124**
Long Term Liabilities				
Notes payable - Banks	169,000			
Noted payable - Other				
Accrued Taxes				
Capital Leases				
Other				
Total Long Term Liabilities		-	-	-
Total Liabilities	**177,448**	**458,157**	**271,636**	**261,124**
Stockholder's Equity	**799,947**	**171,453**	**546,689**	**291,352**
Total Assets and Liabilities	**977,395**	**629,610**	**818,325**	**552,476**

Comparative Income Statements (re-cast)

The following reflects the comparative income statements (with adjustments) to support the figures used in the various valuation methods.

Adjusted Income and Expense
YE 12/31

Year	Thru 6/30 2002	2001	2000	1999
Revenue	2,432,272	5,378,112	4,576,142	3,195,680
Cost of Sales:				
Beginning Inventories		40,000	32,100	22,600
Purchases	1,545,125	4,302,315	3,579,752	2,230,041
Labor		900	420	274
less Ending Inventories	-	(60,000)	(40,000)	(32,100)
Cost of Sales Total	1,545,125	4,283,215	3,572,272	2,220,815
Gross Profit	887,147	1,094,897	1,003,870	974,865
Total Expenses	375,531	765,628	688,961	656,277
Income Before Taxes	**511,616**	**329,269**	**314,909**	**318,588**
Adjustments:				
Officer's Compensation	33,261	145,000	148,000	122,000
Depreciation		12,906	9,384	10,482
Interest	2,002	20,000	24,500	21,250
Total Adjustments	35,263	177,906	181,884	153,732
Net Expenses	340,268	587,722	507,077	502,545
Discretionary Earnings *	**546,879**	**507,175**	**496,793**	**472,320**
Adjusted EBIT **	485,379	388,675	378,293	353,820
EBITD ***	452,118	388,675	378,293	353,820
EBIT ****	485,379	375,769	368,909	343,338

* Dollars available for new owner's compensation, acquisition debt service, actual depreciation reserves and return on invested capital.
** Adjusted EBIT = Earnings Before Interest, Taxes plus Depreciation and Adjustments (less an Appropriate Owner/Manager salary)
*** Earnings B4 Interest, Taxes and Depreciation
**** Earnings B4 Interest and Taxes

Adjusted Balance Sheet

The following documents the adjusted balance sheet to reflect an estimate of the fair market values of the assets and liabilities of the company. Assets and liabilities that might be transferable to a buyer (i.e. available for sale) vs. those that will be retained (i.e. will not be sold) have been segregated.

Assets	Book Value	Adjustment	FMV Transferable Assets	FMV Retained Assets
Cash	155,118			155,118
Marketable Securities	-			-
Accounts Receivable	354,331	124,669		479,000
Inventories	60,000	315,000	375,000	
Prepaid Expenses	-			-
Computer Equipment	-	75,000	75,000	
Equipment and Machinery	140,931	(125,931)	15,000	
Vehicles	-	45,000	45,000	
Office Equipment	-		5,000	
CV of Officer Life Ins.	-	-		-
FMV of Transferable Assets			515,000	
FMV Value of Retained Assets				634,118

Liabilities	Book Value	Adjustment	Transferable Liabilities	Retained Liabilities
Accounts Payable	277,157			277,157
Accrued Profit Sharing	-			-
Accrued Taxes	-			-
Current Portion LT Debt	181,000			181,000
Line of Credit	-			-
Notes to Shareholders	-			-
Notes payable - Banks	-			-
Noted payable - Other	-			-
Accrued Taxes	-			-
Capital Leases	-			-
Other	-			-
Book Value of Liabilities	458,157			
Value of Transferable Liabilities			-	
Value of Retained Liabilities				458,157
Residual Value				**175,961**

Ratio Analysis

The following outlines the various analyses performed to evaluate the financial health of the business. Each analysis is used to view a different segment of the business from a financial and operational perspective. These analyses were used to support the conclusions derived at the end of this report.

- · Comparative operating ratio review
- · Return on investment
- · Safety and liquidity
- · Operating efficiency

Comparative operating ratio review

This exhibit reviews the operating history of the company. This information is often used to project future levels of profitability.

Year	2001	2000	1999
Sales	5,378,112	4,576,142	3,195,680
Growth over prior year	18%	43%	
Growth since 1999 (base year)	68%	43%	
Cost of Sales	4,283,215	3,572,272	2,220,815
Ratio	79.6%	78.1%	69.5%
Period Average	76.6%		
Cost of Goods	4,282,795	3,571,998	2,220,815
Ratio	79.6%	78.1%	69.5%
Period Average	76.6%		
Labor Cost	420	274	–
Ratio	0.0%	0.0%	0.0%
Period Average	0.0%		
Net Expenses	587,722	507,077	502,545
Ratio	10.9%	11.1%	15.7%
Period Average	12.1%		
Income Before Taxes	**329,269**	**314,909**	**318,588**
Ratio	6.1%	6.9%	10.0%
Period Average	7.3%		
Discretionary. Earnings	**507,175**	**496,793**	**472,320**
Ratio	9.4%	10.9%	14.8%
Period Average	11.2%		
Adjusted EBIT	**388,675**	**378,293**	**353,820**
Ratio	7.2%	8.3%	11.1%
Period Average	8.5%		
EBIT	**388,675**	**378,293**	**353,820**
Ratio	7.2%	8.3%	11.1%
Period Average	8.5%		
Officer Compensation	145,000	148,000	122,000
Ratio	2.7%	3.2%	3.8%
Period Average	3.2%		

Sales   Sales have increased year by year. Since 1999, sales have grown
68%. From 1999 to 2000, sales increased by 43%. From 2000 to 2001, sales
increased an additional 18%.

Cost of Goods   Gross margins have not been upheld with the company's growth in
sales. Margins have fluctuated between 31.5% (1999) and 21.4% (2001). Three
potential explanations are:
· Raw material costs from suppliers have increased
· Costs to distribute products to customers have increased
· Prices charged to customers have decreased

The company is not contributing the same level of margins (that it has in the past)
to cover other expenses captured in the net expenses line below. As a result, the
income before taxes reflects a lower % to sales as compared to prior years.

Net Expenses   The company has been able to successfully keep its costs in line
while it has grown over the last 3 years.

Income B4 Taxes   Although the company has increased its sales by 68% since 1999
and 18% since 2000, income before taxes does not reflect the same benefit. As a
result of the decrease in gross margins (noted in the cost of goods sold line item
above), the company does not generate the same level of income as a percentage of
sales. Although sales have increased, a buyer might question the amount of value
that has been built over the past 3 years.

Officer's Comp.   Officer's compensation has not increased dramatically with an
increase in sales over the past 3 years.

Ratios for return on investment

	2001	2000	1999
Return on Equity			
Net Income	329,269	314,909	318,588
Stockholder's Equity	171,453	546,689	291,352
Ratio	192%	58%	109%
Return on Assets			
Net Income	329,269	314,909	318,588
Total Assets	629,610	818,325	552,476
Ratio	52%	38%	58%

Return on equity

Return on equity measures the return on the investment made by a business owner. In other words, what is the % return that an owner is receiving for his/her investment into the business. Return on equity does not account for the "time and effort" spent in the business, solely cash payments into the business. This is an important measure to review as it highlights whether the activities spent in the business are generating a reasonable return for the business owner. Many business owners review this ratio to determine:

o Whether the business is generating a sufficient return compared to other opportunities they would be spending with their time

o Analyze the operations to further improve the ratio and build business value.

The company's return on equity is impacted by your recent withdrawal of money from the company. Therefore, it is difficult to determine the exact return on equity. From our limited information available, the ratio appears more than adequate compared to industry standards.

Return on assets

This ratio measures the return on the gross investment of assets employed in the business. This ratio is particularly relevant to evaluate whether the assets that are used in the business are being used properly to build the business' value. From the information provided above, it appears the ratio is more than adequate compared to industry standards.

Ratios to Measure Safety and Liquidity

	2001	2000	1999
Net Working Capital			
Current Assets	569,449	774,598	507,808
- Current Liabilities	458,157	271,636	261,124
	111,292	*502,962*	*246,684*
Current Ratio			
Current Assets	569,449	774,598	507,808
Current Liabilities	458,157	271,636	261,124
Ratio	*1.24*	*2.85*	*1.94*
Quick Ratio			
Cash, Accts & Notes Receivable	509,449	734,598	475,708
Total Current Liabilities	458,157	271,636	261,124
Ratio	*1.11*	*2.70*	*1.82*
Debt to Equity			
Long-term Debt	0	0	0
Stockholder's Equity	171,453	546,689	291,352
Ratio	*0%*	*0%*	*0%*
Sales/WorkingCapital			
Net Sales	5,378,112	4,576,142	3,195,680
Net Working Capital	111,292	502,962	246,684
Ratio	*48.3*	*9.1*	*13.0*

Net Working Capital   The net working capital figure evaluates whether the business generates sufficient cash to meet its short-term obligations. In other words, it determines how much "excess" cash is being generated to support outside financing (for a potential buyer) or used for investments into equipment and other capital expenditures. As of the end of 2001, the business had net working capital of approximately $111,000 to support other cash needs.

Current Ratio

The current ratio evaluates whether the business has sufficient assets to cover current liabilities. As of the end of 2001, it appeared the current assets are adequate to cover its current liabilities. This ratio should be reviewed in context to the operating efficiency ratios below.

A traditional business should have a minimum of a 1:1 ratio and ideally a 2:1 ratio to cover its current liabilities. With a 1:1 ratio, the business is able to generate just enough cash (from its margins) to cover the expenses it owes its suppliers. As the ratio gets higher (i.e. 2:1 or greater), a company becomes less "cash constrained".

Quick Ratio

The quick ratio starts with the current assets and removes inventory to determine whether what is left over can cover the current liabilities. This tends to be what is called an "acid test" to eliminate the impact of slower moving inventory and to see if the current assets continue to support the current liabilities. Based on the information provided, the business appears to be able to cover its current liabilities. One would expect the quick ratio to drop in comparison to the current ratio as inventory has been removed from the mix. If the quick ratio dropped below 1.0, there would be some concern. This does not appear to be the case with your business.

Debt to Total Equity

The debt to total equity ratio evaluates the company's leverage position (i.e. amounts owed to third parties). The company has not extended itself in loans and therefore does not have the financial pressure to service excessive debt payments to third parties.

Sales to Working Capital

The sales to working capital ratio outlines the extent potential creditors are protected by the margin generated.

Ratios Measuring Operating Efficiency

		2001	2000	1999
Collection Period				
Accounts Receivable		354,331	501,705	392,870
Daily sales		14,939	12,712	8,877
	days	23.7	39.5	44.3
# of Days Inventory				
Inventory		350,000	350,000	350,000
Daily cost of Goods		11,897	9,922	6,169
	days	29.4	35.3	56.7
Inventory Turns				
Cost of Goods		4,282,315	3,571,852	2,220,541
Inventory		350,000	350,000	350,000
	times	12.2	10.2	6.3
Cost of Sales/Payables				
Cost of Goods		4,282,315	3,571,852	2,220,541
Payables		277,157	88,951	79,939
	times	15.5	40.2	27.8
# Days Payable				
Payables		277,157	88,951	79,939
Daily Cost of Goods		11,897	9,922	6,169
	days	23.3	9.0	13.0

Collection period   Collection period tells you how long it takes to collect outstanding accounts receivables. From our experience, the following outlines general categories that result from collection periods.

30-35 days	Business has healthy and strong relationships with its customers
45-60 days	Business may not have good collection procedures and/or the value perceived by the customer may be in question
60-90 days	Business is having difficulty collecting receivables and may be heading into financial trouble
90-120 days	Business is in financial trouble

Most companies that operate efficiently have a collection period between 30-35 days, on average. In 2001, the company appears to have collected its receivable balances within a reasonable period of time.

| **# days inventory** | The # of days inventory tells you how many days that you keep inventory around. The # of days in inventory varies by industry. From our experience, the following outlines general categories that result from # days inventory. |

30-45 days	Business is moving inventory at a relatively healthy pace
50-90 days	The business may not be moving inventory regularly
100-120+	Parts of the inventory may become obsolete. An inventory count should be performed to evaluate the status of the inventory.

An efficient company tends to move inventory every 30-45 days. Since the inventory value is not updated on a regular basis, it is difficult to determine whether the inventory is turning on a regular basis. From estimates provided from you it appears inventory exists approximately 30 days, on average, which is a healthy level of inventory turns.

| **# days payable** | The # days payable tells you how often the business is paying supplier invoices. From our experience, the following outlines general categories that result from # days in inventory. |

30-35 days	Supplier relationships appear strong
45-60 days	Business is beginning to strain suppliers
60-90 days	The quality of the business' supplier relationships are in question

Most companies that operate efficiently pay suppliers within a 30-45 day time frame. The company appears to be paying supplier invoices within a healthy time frame.

Asset values

Cost To Replace

Purchasers routinely estimate the costs of creating a similar enterprise when considering the purchase of an existing business. It provides one point of reference to estimate the amount incurred to replace the assets of the business.

	Book Value	Estimated Cost to Replace
Inventories	60,000	375,000
Prepaid Expenses	-	5,000
Computer	-	150,000
Equipment and Machinery	140,931	25,000
Vehicles	-	80,000
Office Equipment	-	10,000
Organizational Expenses	-	2,500
Other	-	
Estimated Cost to Replace	$	**647,500**

Liquidation value

This exhibit estimates the liquidation values of the Company's assets. Lenders routinely use this value when calculating collateral values for lending purposes.

	Fair Market Value	Liquidation Factor	Liquidation Value
Cash	155,118	1.00	155,118
Marketable Securities	-	1.00	-
Accounts Receivable	479,000	0.95	455,050
Inventories	375,000	0.90	337,500
Prepaid Expenses	-	0.90	-
Computer Equipment	75,000	0.20	15,000
Equipment and Machinery	15,000	0.70	10,500
Vehicles	45,000	0.90	40,500
Office Equipment	-	0.25	-
CV of Officer Life Ins.	-	0.50	-
Estimated Liquidation Value			**1,013,668**

Collateral value of transferable assets

This exhibit is used to estimate the collateral that can be obtained from an outside lender using percentages that lenders traditionally use to finance transactions. In this example, 80% of the equipment and machinery liquidation value might be able to be financed.

	Liquidation Value	Usual % Loan to Value	Collateral Value
Accounts Receivable	455,050	0.00	-
Inventories	337,500	0.80	270,000
Prepaid Expenses	-	0.00	-
Computer Equipment	15,000	0.70	10,500
Equipment and Machinery	10,500	0.80	8,400
Vehicles	40,500	0.90	36,450
Office Equipment	-	0.50	-
CV of Officer Life Ins.	-	0.80	-
Estimated Collateral Value		$	**325,350**

* Assets being retained, not part of sale

Valuation

Introduction

A business is defined as an organized method of routinely producing revenues over a period of time; and fair market value, as stated by the Internal Revenue Service in Revenue Ruling 59-60, is "the price at which property would change hands between a willing buyer and a willing seller when the former is not under compulsion to buy and the latter is not under compulsion to sell; both parties having reasonable knowledge of relevant facts".

The worth of a business can be divided into two major categories:
1. The asset value - machinery, equipment, building, land, usable stock, and other legal rights
2. The business/goodwill value - the premium, over asset value, which a buyer will pay for the organization, historically recorded cash flows, and projected future earnings

Factors that play a part in determining a business's value include:
o   The market value of assets
o   The value of rights, privileges, and knowledge.
o   Historic trends, along with future projections of revenues, expenses, and cash flows.
o   The perception of risk associated with the quality and continuity of earnings.
o   The type or class of buyer that can be attracted to the opportunity and their perception of the opportunity represented.
o   Aesthetic appeal

The techniques and formulas that will be used in arriving at values are those which are generally accepted by business buyers and their professional advisors.

The results assume the buyer and seller are considering alternative investments, so that a transaction occurs when the economic incentive to purchase is equal to the economic incentive to sell.

Generally, there is no economic incentive to invest monies in a business that is not capable of producing a net income in excess of both an operator's salary and a reasonable return on invested capital.

The application of financial formulas is generally straightforward. However, it must be recognized that the marketplace is made up of many buyers and that each can make an estimate of value that may be generous or conservative depending upon perceptions of a range of criteria.

Allowing for these differences is not always straightforward, since feeling, desires, and judgments must be quantified. Such considerations result in calculations that must take probability into account.
And so, a proper valuation will develop a range of values that indicates how the marketplace of the different buyers and investors is likely to view the business. This range suggests the highest price a seller can expect, and the lowest price a seller should accept.

Value

It must be clearly understood that, in all cases, values discussed do not presume any buyer assumption of the Company's debt, liabilities, and obligations that might exist at the time of a sale. All such items must be acknowledged as the responsibility of the ownership. It should be mentioned, however, that with proper planning, some items of debt and liability can be addressed as a part of the acquisition process.

In this same regard, it must be clear that the value of certain assets will flow directly to management from the company, rather than from the acquirer. These will presumably include company vehicles, cash and accounts receivable.

Methods and Techniques

There is a wide array of methods and techniques that can be utilized to value a business.   Among those considered and not applied, were:
  - o   Capitalization of Profits
  - o   Rothschild Banking Formula
  - o   Multiples of Revenue
  - o   Rules of Thumb
  - o   Comparison with Public Company Transactions

The approaches selected were deemed appropriate because of the history, size, and profile of the Company, and the segments of the marketplace that might participate in its purchase.

These approaches acknowledge asset value but more importantly, focus upon adjusted cash flows, excess earnings, return on investment, and capacity to carry debt.

Marketplace

The current marketplace for companies is made up, essentially, of four types of acquirers. An outline description of each is as follows:

1. The Strategic Acquirer
   o Typically a large firm, usually a Public Company
   o Accustomed to long term planning
   o Economic considerations are evaluated; however, reason for acquisition is not always purely economic
   o Acquisition prompted by factors such as establishing new markets

2. The Corporate or Sophisticated Acquirer
   o Typically comes from a large company background
   o Employs "schooled" approach when determining value
   o Usually a high net worth individual, a group of individuals, an investor group, or a small Corporation
   o Focuses on current and future, rather than past
   o Places primary emphasis on capitalization of earnings, and on the ability to finance and leverage a purchase

3. The Financial or Lifestyle Buyer
   o Usually an individual
   o Primary focus on income replacement and the opportunity to build equity
   o Major emphasis placed on historic and current conditions
   o Case for case, the perception of risk is likely to be higher than that of the strategic or corporate style acquirer

4. The Industry or Asset Buyer
   o Usually from within the same, or affiliated, field as the company
   o Primary focus is on a business's fixed assets
   o Presumes that they will bring virtually all other value to the enterprise

The following sections address value from the varying perspectives of these buyers.

Industry or Asset Buyer Method

Book Value, Adjusted Book Value, Liquidation Value Methods

Industry and other asset-focused buyers will predictably perform an analysis of the value of transferable assets. Therefore they use the book value, adjusted book value and liquidation value of the assets to place a value on the opportunity. The book value method uses the value placed on the books and records to establish a value. The adjusted book value simply adjusts the book value to the fair market value. The liquidation value estimates the amount that could be raised by selling off the transferable assets. Given your industry, we weighted the most probable method that will be used to establish a value on the transferable assets.

	Book Value	Book Value Adjusted to FMV	Liquidation Value
Inventories	60,000	375,000	337,500
Equipment and Machinery	140,931	15,000	10,500
Vehicles	-	45,000	40,500
Office Equipment	-	5,000	-
	-	-	-
Less Depreciation	(80,770)		
Book Value $	**120,161**		
Adjusted Book Value		$ 440,000	
Liquidation Value			$ 388,500

Methods	Values	*Summary* Weight	Extension
Book Value	120,161	0.00	-
Adjusted Book Value	440,000	1.00	440,000
Liquidation Value	388,500	0.00	-
	948,661	1.00	440,000
Straight Average	316,220		
Weighted Average		440,000	
Probable Asset Buyer Value		$	**440,000**

Financial Buyer Methods

Financial buyers (and their advisors) will review historic financial performance in an effort to obtain a level of comfort as to probable earnings levels available to them for: a salary for the new owner, acquisition debt service and, replacement reserves. This exhibit displays the computations most often employed for this purpose and estimates results of the exercise.

There are 5 different valuation methods that are traditionally used by Financial Buyers. These follow and, where appropriate, use the calculations from this exercise within those methods.

	Discretionary Earnings	Weight	Extension
2001	507,175	3	1,521,525
2000	496,793	2	993,586
1999	472,320	1	472,320
Totals	1,476,288	6	2,987,431
Most recent year	507,175		
Straight Average			369,072
Weighted Average			497,905

Estimate of earnings that a Financial Buyer will perceive as available for acquisition $ 500,000

Basic Method

This method combines the two major elements of business value to calculate worth. The first method adds perceived earnings and assets at current market value. The second formula is essentially the same but considers the Barrier of Entry and uses up to two years of Discretionary Earnings to address the time required to start a business and bring it to a similar cash position. Two years is generally the maximum time period buyers are willing to use.

First Method			
Fair Market Value of Assets		515,000	
plus			
One year Discretionary Earnings		500,000	
Resultant Value		**1,015,000**	
Second Method			
Fair Market Value of Assets		515,000	
plus			
Monthly Earning	41,667		
multiplied by # months to reach			
same level of profitability	24	1,000,000	
Resultant Value		**1,515,000**	
Average both methods to obtain Basic Value			
Basic Method Value		**$**	**1,265,000**

Comparable Sales Method

The comparable sales method uses sales data from hundreds of completed transactions to derive the sale price and down payment ratios. These ratios are then applied to the subject company to derive estimated values.

Sale Price Ratios	Ratios	Down Payment Ratios	Ratios
Sale Price/Revenues	0.35	Down Pay/Revenues	0.15
Sale Price/Disc. Earnings	2.37	Down Pay/Disc. Earnings	1.02
Sale Price/Asset Value (FMV)	1.64	Down Pay/Asset Value (FMV)	0.71

Subject Business:		
Revenues	$	4,576,142
Discretionary Earnings		500,000
FMV Assets		515,000

Ratios applied to subject business

Sale Price	Weight	Extension	Down Payment	Weight	Extension
SP/Revenues	2	3,203,299	DP/Revenues	2	1,372,843
SP/Disc. Earnings	1	1,185,000	DP/Disc. Earnings	1	510,000
SP/Asset Value (FMV)	0	-	DP/Asset Value (FMV)	0	-
Totals	3	4,388,299		3	1,882,843

Probable Down Payment $ **627,614**

Probable Sale Price $ **1,462,766**

Discretionary Earnings Method

This method addresses the three prime considerations of a Financial or Lifestyle Buyer: Transaction financing, salary or wage and a return on invested capital. Discretionary Earnings are reduced for debt service and an appropriate return on investment or cost of capital. The result produces an amount approximating the down payment, typically 1/3 of the purchase price.

Discretionary Earnings Method

This method addresses the three prime considerations of a Financial or Lifestyle Buyer :
1) Transaction financing, 2) a salary or wage and, 3) a return on invested capital. Discretionary Earnings are reduced for debt service and an appropriate return on investment or cost of capital. The result produces an amount approximating the down payment, typically 1/3 of the purchase price.

Discretionary Earnings	$	500,000
less 25% reserved for debt service	X	0.75
Buyer's expected wage or earnings		375,000
less Return on Investment (ROI) 10%	-	37,500
Buyer's net cash advantage		337,500
Divide by typical down payment of 33%	=	1,022,727

Resultant Discretionary Earnings Value	**$**	**1,022,727**

Cost to Replace

Most Financial Buyers will balance a sale price against their perception of the cost to create a similar business from scratch. This exhibit reflects an estimate of the replacement cost of the transferable assets of the business.

Inventories	375,000
Prepaid Expenses	5,000
Computer	150,000
Equipment and Machinery	25,000
Vehicles	80,000
Office Equipment	10,000
Organizational Expenses	2,500
Other	-
Estimated Cost to Replace Value	$ 647,500

Debt Capacity Method

Discretionary Earnings are reduced by:

- o An appropriate owner/manager salary
- o Actual depreciation reserves to determine earnings available for Debt Service

The value produced represents the level of debt this business could service given the current level of earnings.

Discretionary Earnings	$	500,000
less Owner/Manager Salary		118,500
less Depreciation/Replacement Reserves		50,000
Dollars available for Debt Service		331,500
Assumptions:		
Interest Rate	9.0%	
Term of Note (yrs)	7	
Monthly Payment $	27,625	
Probable Debt Capacity Value		**$1,717,003**
Preliminary estimates of value by SBA lenders indicates their opinion of Value ranges between $1,600,000 and $1,717,500		

Summary of All Values – Financial Buyer Methods

This exhibit shows the results produced by the various methods likely to be employed by the Financial Buyer and weights them as to probability of use, producing a summary value.

Methods	Values	Weight	Extension
Basic	1,265,000	0.05	63,250
Discretionary Earnings	1,022,727	0.05	51,136
Comparable Sales	1,462,766	0.40	585,107
Cost to Replace	647,500	-	-
Debt Capacity	1,717,003	0.50	858,502
	6,114,997	1.00	1,557,995
Straight Average Value	1,222,999		
Weighted Average Value	1,557,995		
Target Value		$	**1,500,000**

Convert Fair Market Value to Fair Cash Value – Financial Buyer Methods

Fair Market Value (FMV) is universally defined as a price received in "cash or equivalent." However, because financing for the acquisition of small and mid size businesses is restricted, the American Society of Appraisers (ASA) has redefined FMV for business transfers as "the price received under terms usual in the marketplace" i.e. Seller Financing. This exhibit measures the impact of restrictive financing and demands for a cash transaction and converts the Sophisticated Buyer's terms price to Fair Cash Value. It must be noted that the down payment typically is limited to $300,000 or less if the buyer is an individual.

Target Purchase Price	$	1,500,000
Usual Down Payment (20%)		300,000
Probable Bank Loan		1,000,000
Possible Cash at Transfer		1,300,000
Usual Seller's Note		200,000
Total Price (FMV)		1,500,000

1) Unfinanced portion of Transaction	13.3%
2) Divide by 2, add result to CAP rate as an adder for lack of financing	6.7%
3) CAP Rate for this business	34.8%
4) Discount Rate	41.5%

5) Apply Discount Rate to usual Seller's Note to calculate Present Value

	Annual note payments:	Present Value Factor	Present Value of Payments
1st year	52,759	0.706880	37,295
2nd year	52,759	0.499680	26,363
3rd year	52,759	0.353214	18,635
4th year	52,759	0.249680	13,173
5th year	52,759	0.176494	9,312

6) Present Value of usual Seller's Note	104,778
7) Add Cash at Transfer	1,300,000
Estimated Fair Cash Value	**1,404,778**

Justification of Purchase and Transaction Structure
(Financial Buyer)

Financial and Lifestyle Buyers generally expect the ratio of living wage to down payment to range between 70% and 90%. When the ratio drops below 70% our database of actual sales indicates that a transaction is unlikely to occur.

Example: The Financial Buyer with a down payment of $100K will typically expect a living wage of between $70K and $90K be available after debt service and replacement reserves.

Assumptions:	Seller's Note	Bank Note
Interest Rate	8.0%	8.0%
# Years Note	7.0	7.0
# Years Covenant not to Compete	5.0	
# Years Consulting Agreement	5.0	
The Ratios under this scenario equal:	**79.7%**	**35.6%**

Possible Structure:	Terms	Cash
Target Purchase Price	1,500,000	1,404,778
Down Payment	300,000	1,404,778
Covenant not to Compete	50,000	
Consulting Agreement		
Bank Note	1,000,000	
Seller's Note	150,000	
Total Purchase Price	1,500,000	

Annual Debt Service:		
Covenant not to Compete	10,000	
Consulting Agreement	-	
Bank Note	192,072	
Seller's Note	28,811	
Total Debt Service	230,883	

Discretionary Earnings	500,000	500,000
less Debt Service	(230,883)	
less Return on Buyer's Cash Down	(30,000)	
Earnings available for Owner's Compensation and Depreciation reserves	$ 239,117	$ 500,000

Sophisticated Buyer Methods

Sophisticated Buyers (and their advisors) will use various methods in determining the amount of earnings available for the transaction. A review of historic results and their perception of the opportunity will flavor their conclusions. Note that projections are taken into account and an Owner/Manager's wage is deducted from Discretionary Earnings (Adjusted EBIT).

Year	Adjusted EBIT	Wgt	Extension	Wgt	Extension
2006	1,103,637			1	1,103,637
2005	944,900			2	1,889,799
2004	786,162			3	2,358,486
2003	627,425			4	2,509,699
Est. Current Yr.	565,556	2	1,131,112	5	2,827,780
2001	388,675	5	1,943,375	5	1,943,375
2000	378,293	4	1,513,172	4	1,513,172
1999	353,820	3	1,061,460	3	1,061,460
	1,120,788	14	5,649,119	27	15,207,408

Most recent yr.	388,675
3 Year Straight average	373,596
Weighted average	403,508
Weighted historic and future average	563,237
Estimated Current Year	565,556
Estimated First Year	627,425

Estimate of earnings that a Sophisticated Buyer will perceive as available for acquisition $ **600,000**

There are traditionally 6 valuation methods used by the "Sophisticated buyer". These valuation methods follow.

Excessive Earnings Method

This method blends the values of assets and earnings to determine the value of a business. A portion of Adjusted EBIT is assigned as a return on money invested in company assets. The remainder is defined as Excess Earnings and is regarded as having been generated by the company's intangible assets - mainly goodwill. These Excess Earnings are then capitalized and added to the FMV of assets being acquired to produce a total value for all the tangible and intangible components of the business.

Adjusted EBIT		$ 600,000
Fair Market Value of Transferable Assets	440,000	
Times investment rate	15.0%	
Equals return on investment in company assets		66,000
Excess earnings		534,000
Capitalize excess earnings @		34.8%
Produces a value for the company's intangible assets		1,534,483
Plus FMV of assets being transferred		440,000
Resultant Value		**$ 1,974,483**

Discounted Present Profits

This method projects present earnings over a period of time and then calculates the present value of these earnings. The sum of the discounted earnings represents the present value of the expected future earnings. Present earnings are adjusted at a nominal rate to account for inflation.

Year	Adjusted EBIT	PV Factor 34.8%	Present Value of Earnings	Inflation Rate
1	600,000	0.741840	445,104	2.0%
2	612,000	0.550326	336,800	
3	624,240	0.408254	254,848	
4	636,725	0.302859	192,838	
5	649,459	0.224673	145,916	
Discounted Future Earnings Value			**$ 1,375,506**	

Discounted Projected Earnings

This method, sometimes referred to as "Present Value of Future Earnings," uses projected earnings for a period of time and then calculates the present value of these earnings. The sum of the discounted earnings represents the present value of the expected future earnings.

End Year	Adjusted EBIT	Present Value Factor 34.8%	Present Value of Earnings
1	627,425	0.741840	465,449
2	786,162	0.550326	432,646
3	944,900	0.408254	385,759
4	1,103,637	0.302859	334,246
5	1,262,374	0.224673	283,621
	Discounted Projected Earnings Value	$	**1,901,721**

Multiple of EBIT Methods

EBIT methods are widely used and misused by many Sophisticated Buyers. EBIT and EBITD methods may be inappropriate for many small and mid size companies as a significant amount of earnings generally have been recorded as discretionary expenses.

	Type EBIT		Range of Multiple	Range of Value		
1)	Adjusted EBIT	388,675	2	777,350		
			3	1,166,025		
			4	1,554,700		
	Appropriate Multiple		3.5			
	Probable Adjusted EBIT Value				$	1,360,363
2)	EBITD		3	1,166,025		
		388,675	4	1,554,700		
			5	1,943,375		
	Appropriate Multiple		5			
	Probable EBITD Value				$	1,943,375
3)	EBIT		4	1,503,076		
		375,769	5	1,878,845		
			6	2,254,614		
			7	2,630,383		
	Appropriate Multiple		6			
	Probable EBIT Value				$	2,254,614

Summary of EBIT Values:		Weight		
EBIT-DA	1,360,363	2	2,720,725	
EBITD	1,943,375	2	3,886,750	
EBIT	2,254,614	1	2,254,614	
	5,558,352	5.00	8,862,089	
Straight Average	1,852,784			
	Weighted Average		1,772,418	
	Probable EBIT Method Value		$	1,800,000

Capitalization of Income

The capitalization of income method takes a number of different earnings figures and applies a capitalization rate to derive a value. Probable weighting factors are applied to the resultant values and summarized to estimate the value from this method.

	Earnings	Cap Rate	Value	Wgt	Extension
Method #1 Capitalize most recent year's earnings	388,675	34.8%	1,116,882	0.20	223,376
Method #2 Capitalize average earnings	373,596	34.8%	1,073,552	0.05	53,678
Method #3 Capitalize weighted average earnings	403,508	34.8%	1,159,507	0.05	57,975
Method #4 Capitalize estimated current year	627,425	34.8%	1,802,944	0.30	540,883
Method #5 Capitalize historic & projected earnings	563,237	34.8%	1,618,498	0.05	80,925
Method #6 Capitalize estimated earnings	600,000	34.8%	1,724,138	0.35	603,448
			8,495,522	1.00	1,560,286
	Straight average		1,415,920		
		Weighted average			1,560,286
Probable Capitalization of Income Value				$	**1,500,000**

SBA Lenders Method

Lenders use several methods to determine a business's approximate value prior to seriously entertaining an acquisition's funding request. The values shown below are a leading SBA lender's initial estimate of this firm's value. Under recent SBA rulings, lending involving a significant component of goodwill (goodwill equals the value in excess of assets) must be justified by external valuation sources. Typically, outside appraisals are required on transactions in excess of $1 million.

Financing Method
Range of Value   1,782,179   up to   1,912,129

Weighted Earnings Method
Range of Value   1,450,704   up to   1,556,485

Weighted Capitalization Method
Range of Value   1,300,078   up to   1,543,843

Overall Lenders Opinion of Value
Range of Value   1,600,778   up to   1,717,602

Probable SBA Lender's Value   **1,650,000**

Summary of Values – Sophisticated Buyer Methods

This exhibit summarizes and weights the various methods as to the probability of use thereby deriving a summary value.

Method	Value	Weight	Extension
Excess Earnings	1,974,483	0.35	691,069
Discounted Present Earnings	1,375,506	0.05	68,775
Discounted Projected Earnings	1,901,721	0.05	95,086
Capitalization of Earnings	1,500,000	0.20	300,000
Multiple of EBIT	1,800,000	0.25	450,000
SBA Lender	1,650,000	0.10	165,000
	10,201,709	1.00	1,769,930
Straight Average Value	1,700,285		
Weighted Average Value	1,769,930		
Target Value		$	**1,750,000**

Convert Fair Market Value to Fair Cash Value – Sophisticated Buyer Methods
Fair Market Value (FMV) is universally defined as a price received in "cash or equivalent." However, because financing for the acquisition of small and mid size businesses is restricted, the American Society of Appraisers (ASA) has redefined FMV for business transfers as "the price received under terms usual in the marketplace" i.e. Seller Financing. This exhibit measures the impact of restrictive financing and demands for a cash transaction and converts the Sophisticated Buyer's terms price to Fair Cash Value. It must be noted that the down payment typically is limited to $300,000 or less if the buyer is an individual.

Target Purchase Price	$	1,750,000
Usual Down Payment		600,000
Probable Bank Loan		1,000,000
Possible Cash at Transfer		1,600,000
Usual Seller's Note		150,000
Total Price (FMV)		1,750,000

1) Unfinanced portion of Transaction 8.6%
2) Divide by 2, add result to CAP rate as
   an adder for lack of financing 4.3%
3) CAP Rate for this business 34.8%
4) Discount Rate 39.1%
5) Apply Discount Rate to usual Seller's Note to calculate Present Value

Annual note payments:		Present Value Factor	Present Value of Payments
1st year	39,570	0.718981	28,450
2nd year	39,570	0.516934	20,455
3rd year	39,570	0.371666	14,707
4th year	39,570	0.267221	10,574
5th year	39,570	0.192127	7,602

6) Present Value of usual Seller's Note 81,788
7) Add Cash at Transfer 1,600,000

Estimated Fair Cash Value   **$ 1,681,788**

Justification of Purchase and Transaction Structure
(Sophisticated Buyer)

Corporate or Sophisticated Acquirers - will deduct an appropriate manager's salary, debt service and reserves for depreciation from Discretionary Earnings and then calculate the return on their initial investment (ROI). The ROI should approximate the capitalization rate developed as a measure of risk appropriate to the opportunity (plus or minus 10%).

Example: Discretionary Earnings of $350K less an appropriate owner/manager salary divided by the initial investment will produce an ROI percentage.

	$350K	Discretionary Earnings
less	250K	Salary, Debt service and Depreciation Reserves
equals	$100K	$ Return on Investment (ROI)
divided by	400K	Down Payment
equals	25%	% Return on Investment (ROI)

Assumptions:	Seller's Note	Bank Note
Interest Rate	8%	8.0%
# Years Note	5	5
# Years Covenant not to Compete	5	
# Years Consulting Agreement	5	

The Capitalization Rate developed for this company is:		34.8%
The Ratio under this scenario equal:	42.0%	15.0%
Possible Structure:	Terms	Cash
Target Purchase Price	$ 1,750,000	1,681,788
Down Payment	600,000	1,681,788
Bank Loan	1,000,000	
Covenant not to Compete	-	
Consulting Agreement	-	
Seller's Note	150,000	
Total Purchase Price	1,750,000	
Annual Debt Service:		
Covenant not to Compete	-	
Consulting Agreement	-	
Seller's Note	37,568	
Bank Note	250,456	
Total Debt Service	288,025	
Adjusted EBIT	600,000	
less Debt Service	(288,025)	
less Return on Buyer's Cash Down	(60,000)	
Buyer's Return on invested capital	$ 251,975	$ 600,000

Strategic Plan

This section is organized to summarize the work performed to substantiate the conclusions reached, which buyers would be attracted to this business, favorable news about the company (including the preliminary business value), unfavorable news about the business and the opportunity to further increase value in the company from a buyer's perspective.

Work Effort Performed

Over the course of the last few weeks we have:
·   Researched and reviewed the industry's dynamics
·   Performed a brief assessment of the company's operations
·   Analyzed the financial position of the company
·   Identified the various types of buyers that may be attracted to the business
·   Utilized a number of valuation methods to establish a preliminary business value (from a future buyer's perspective)
·   Evaluated and identified the risks a lender might find in the business that may impact a buyer's ability to finance the operation
·   Estimated the amount of financing available for a potential buyer
·   Identified what appears to be working well in the company ("the favorable news")
·   Highlighted areas that warrant some concern in the business ("the unfavorable news")
·   Documented areas for opportunity to further increase value

As a result, we have been able to develop an opinion on:
·   The potential values that different buyers might bring to the table
·   What a potential buyer might find "attractive" and "unattractive" about the business
·   The amount of financing that may/may not get raised from an outside lender, using your business as collateral, and the amount that might be requested for a seller's note
·   What to do to further increase your business's value
·   Options available to you going forward

Summary of Key Questions

The key questions that need to be answered are:
1.   Who is the "Right" Buyer?
2.   How much might a potential buyer pay for the business?
3.   What is the opportunity for a potential buyer?
4.   What can be done to increase the value of the business?
5.   What could the value potentially grow to?
6.   Should I put my business up for sale (a personal decision)?
7.   In summary, what are the options to pursue?

1. Who is the "Right" Buyer?

Within our analysis, we reviewed each type of buyer to determine the "right" buyer. We developed different valuation methods by each type of buyer to determine which buyer might pay the most amount of money for your business. With the understanding that there are many different types of valuation methods, different types of buyers will use different methods to substantiate the value of the business. For each relevant buyer, we have calculated what each type of buyer may establish as a value. As a result, we determined:

- **A Strategic acquirer would most likely <u>not be attracted</u> to this business**
  A strategic acquirer is a firm that tends to be greater than $75 million in revenue. This types of buyer is attracted to businesses that:
  - Have proprietary processes they can learn from and leverage
  - Enable them to reduce their own costs
  - Let them sell products through their existing channels and vice versa
  - Provide an opportunity to own new technology
  - Have a minimum of $20 million in revenues

- **An Industry buyer will most likely <u>not pay the highest price</u> for this business.**
  An Industry buyer is often confused with a Strategic acquirer. Industry buyers lack strategic or synergistic motivations for purchasing a company. Unlike Strategic acquirers (who focus on future benefits of technologies and market share) Industry buyers generally focus only upon selected assets and resist acknowledging a company's intangible value or "Goodwill." You might not get the highest price possible marketing the business toward an Industry buyer. In most situations this buyer is the buyer of last resort. Exceptions occurs when:
  - A company's earnings are not commensurate with invested capital or,
  - The operational skills are not readily transferable and the firm lacks a sufficient infrastructure to continue without the present owner.

- **A Corporate or Sophisticated Buyer is most likely the <u>buyer of choice</u>.**
  Corporate or Sophisticated buyers are often the buyer of choice as they regularly take future earnings into account when assessing value. This allows you to maximize your value. However, to attract this type of buyer, prospects for future growth and profitability must be documented with credible and supportable assumptions.

- **A Financial buyer may be used as <u>a second option.</u>**
  The Financial buyer may find the Company attractive, however, this buyer would need significant training and assistance from existing management as part of the purchase price. Additionally, this buyer's perception of risk would have a limiting effect on initial capital investments and heighten requests for significant levels of seller financing.

How much might a potential buyer pay for the business?

· *In its current state, a Corporate or Sophisticated buyer might pay up to $1,750,000 for the business (with terms).*

Below is a summary of values that was derived through a number of different valuation methods by different types of buyers. As noted above, the Strategic Acquirer would not have an interest in this type of business and therefore the following table does not reflect this buyer's value estimate.

Industry or Asset Buyer Methods	Values	Weight	Extension	
Book Value	120,161	-	-	
Adjusted Book Value	440,000	1.00	440,000	
Liquidation Value	388,500	-	-	
		1.00		
Probable Asset Buyer Value			$	**440,000**
Financial or Lifestyle Buyer Methods				
Basic	1,265,000	0.05	63,250	
Discretionary Earnings	1,022,727	0.05	51,136	
Comparable Sales	1,462,766	0.40	585,107	
Cost to Replace	647,500	-	-	
Debt Capacity	1,717,003	0.50	858,502	
		1.00		
Probable Financial Buyer Value			$	**1,500,000**
Estimated Cash Value	$	**1,404,778**		
Sophisticated or Corporate Buyer Methods				
Excess Earnings	1,974,483	0.25	691,069	
Discounted Present Earnings	1,375,506	0.05	68,775	
Discounted Projected Earnings	1,901,721	0.05	95,086	
Capitalization of Earnings	1,500,000	0.20	300,000	
Multiple of EBIT	1,800,000	0.25	450,000	
SBA Lender	1,650,000	0.10	165,000	
		1.00		
Probable Sophisticated Buyer Value			$	**1,750,000**
Estimated Cash Value	$	**1,681,788**		
Target Value			$	**1,750,000**

Based on our analysis, we believe that the business in its current state could attract a Corporate or Sophisticated buyer. He/she is the most likely buyer of choice and will pay up to $1,750,000 for the business. He/she would most likely request you to take back a seller's note and also be involved in the business for a transition period. This value is derived from many assumptions that are embedded in this report's analysis. Please refer to the analysis and assumptions for further details.

Through our review, as noted above, we also analyzed the financial position of the company enabling us to determine some of the valued elements of the business as well as areas that may appear to be "risky" to a potential buyer. Based on our knowledge of the markets, industry, buyer perceptions, etc. we prepared a high-level risk assessment of your industry and your operations. Through this assessment we were able to further uncover items that are of value and/or may warrant further attention.

Finally, we have outlined (ahead of time) the "favorable news" and the "unfavorable news" that a buyer will raise during a potential sale of a business. We find buyers have certain expectations of companies they seek to purchase. Many times for companies, the "favorable news" is expected. The "unavorable news" creates some red flags. Depending on the type of buyer and his/her experiences, a he/she might become wary of the "not so good news", question the business value and attempt to negotiate the price down. These are outlined as follows:

Good News – A buyer will find:

o *You have a strong financial position*
The company appears to be in relatively strong financial health. We reviewed the various financial ratios of the business including its yearly comparative ratios, liquidity ratios and operating efficiencies. From our review, we were able to determine:
   - The company has upheld its revenues over the past 3 years
   - The company has a strong cash flow
   - Average collection periods are <u>within</u> acceptable standards
   - The # of days payables outstanding are better than standards in the industry
   - From peripheral information, it appears, inventory is moving through your operation at a healthy rate
   - Average margins are healthy overall
   - Current assets are sufficient to cover current liabilities and meet short-term obligations
   - The company is not highly leveraged and does not have the burdens of servicing debt

o *There is a loyal customer base*
A potential buyer will value the steady stream of revenue that comes into the Company. The buyer will find that virtually no one customer accounts for more than 5% of the total sales.

o *You have a broad product offering*
The types of products you offer in the market place appear to be well diversified and complimentary to each other to cross sell products and/or services to your customers. As a result, a buyer would find it attractive that he/she might be able to further sell the products into the existing customer base. A buyer will also value that the business is not solely reliant on one product.

o *You can compete more effectively with the integrated supplier arrangements*
A potential buyer will value your integrated supply arrangements. A buyer might view this as the business having "power" over both the competition and your customers. Without these integrated supply arrangements, your competitors do not have the breadth of products to offer the marketplace. Customers have become more reliant upon you as a one-stop-shop that provides a reliable service. A buyer would value this aspect of your business. Assuming service levels remain high and the business continues to be able to offer the variety of products to the marketplace, a customer would need a compelling reason to go to a competitor. You have leverage over your subcontractors as well. By having the primary relationships with your customers, you "feed" your subcontractors work making them dependent on you for revenue. This places you more in the "driver's seat" than one of your competitors that do not have an integrated supply arrangement.
Finally, by having orders drop shipped directly to customers, the costs of handling, etc. is virtually eliminated, dropping directly to the bottom line thereby creating value in the business.

o *Value in the PPPPP relationship*
Brand awareness, the volume of product distributed and the margins generated is all that will matter to a potential buyer. As long as these 3 variables are maintained and mixed well, a potential buyer will place some value on the relationship.

o *You are not dependent on one supplier*
A buyer will value the fact that you have many product lines with a number of suppliers to source product from. From a buyer's perspective this reduces the overall risk of a supplier "shutting" off its supply of product to you.

o *There is not a heavy capital investment into new equipment required*
Much of your equipment is functional and does not require replacement. A buyer will value that he/she does not have to incur further cash outlays to upgrade equipment, etc.

o *The Company has a good reputation*
A buyer will value the fact that the Company has been in existence for over 50 years. The name is well recognized in the market place and has a dominant position in the local market among competitors of equal size.

o *Margin generated through subcontractors is healthy*
The margin that you generate through your integrated supplier arrangements and drop shipped orders is attractive to a potential buyer. Assuming this can be maintained and/or automated will increase your attractiveness.

"Unfavorable News" - A buyer will find:
- *The industry is not positioned for aggressive growth in the next 5 years*
  Based on the research we conducted, we determined the industry might grow between 3-4% between 2002 and 2008. Most buyers (ones that are not in the industry) tend to look for businesses that grow a <u>minimum</u> of 5-7% per year.

- *The revenues are not well diversified among many industries*
  Although you do service the Manufacturing, Construction, State and Local Government, Healthcare, and Bio-Technology sectors, it is no secret that your business is heavily reliant (almost 50% of the revenues) on State related business. With the contract up for renewal at the end of the year, a potential buyer would question whether revenues are sustainable for the longer term. Even if the contract is established, a buyer might still question whether the contract is a "guarantee" of future revenues. A contract that does not have a provision where a minimum amount of requisitions get purchased through the Company may appear as a risk to a potential buyer.

  Excluding the State business, the top 10 customers represent approximately 35% of the business. Should one customer from this top 10 list go to a competitor, it could have an impact to the bottom line.

- *You are operationally constrained*
  There is not much room to expand in your current space. The warehouse is virtually at capacity and there is no physical space to expand inside or outside of the building. Should a buyer want to increase the product offering, hold more inventory, etc. he/she will be constrained by the current space. By having access to additional space (e.g. public warehouse space), it would alleviate a buyer's impression of "confined quarters" that may not appear to be a "well-run ship", impacting perceived value. When a potential buyer walks into a business, he/she perceives value based on his/her first impression of the business's operations. A clean, organized operation (office, warehouse, files, etc.) makes a big difference in the value perception.

- *There is no formal lease for the property*
  Without a formal lease, a potential buyer might find he/she would have to move from the location in a short period of time requiring him/her to find a new location and incur the moving costs. In addition, the cost of your lease is well below market, potentially impacting a buyer's ability to move and keep overhead costs low (a similar comment is noted below) to generate the same level of cash flow. Should a buyer want to move from the existing space, he/she will be hard pressed to find space that has a similar low cost to lease, impacting his/her flexibility in the business.

o *There is no standard pricing in place*
Based on our analysis, we discovered that pricing is not consistent from person to person having an impact on the bottom line. A potential buyer might view this as losing control over the amount of margin that could be maximized in the business.

o *The business is locally/regionally focused*
A buyer will discover that much of your business is highly local/regional. A buyer may view this as a potential risk whereby a larger, more national player may be able to compete with you on price and service. This does appear unlikely as your relationships with your customers appear strong.

o *Systems and controls do not match companies of a similar size*
Although you do have some systems and controls in place, many companies of similar size have more robust controls to manage the business. Many companies have formalized reporting that is provided to a Management group with financial oversight so they are aware of the critical issues that are occurring in the business (e.g. gross profit margins, sales by customer, incentive systems, etc.). A buyer will quickly uncover the tools that are (or are not) being used to manage the business. Most buyers like to walk into companies that have an established infrastructure (i.e. systems, processes, established routines, controls, periodic reports, etc.). Although buyers understand that the infrastructure will not be designed in context as they see the world, they do expect that the minimum financial and operational data is being produced, reviewed and acted upon on a regular basis. Not even the best of CEOs are able to truly build the most value in a company without access to this type of information.

o *Family is in the business and may remain*
A buyer will appreciate the strong culture that you have developed. Although your family members may like to stay in the business, a buyer might view this as a potential risk as he/she might want to change the operation and might face resistance. We cannot say this would occur, but we have seen buyers' perceptions of value be impacted by this issue.

o *There is no sales force*
A buyer will find that he/she will have to build a sales force. Without a sales force, there is no formal program in place to generate new business. A buyer will have to incur the ramp-up time to hire, train and establish a formal selling program.

2. What is the opportunity for a potential buyer?

Buyers typically do not purchase a business solely for the money that it generates. Buyers want to make the business theirs. They want to instill their mark on the business to reflect their skills and abilities to bring the business to the "next level". Therefore there must be opportunities available to a potential buyer. Some opportunities, certainly not intended to be a complete list, are listed below.

1. Sell products/services into larger accounts
2. Instill better systems and processes
3. Leverage the integrated supplier arrangement model to a national level
4. Leverage the business model toward the web
5. Exploit existing markets with different product lines
6. Consolidate operations into one location (for an existing company in the industry) and close down the facility

3. What can be done to increase the value of the business?

- ○ *Evaluate options of buying another business whose "strengths" are your "areas for development"*

  Based on our analysis, it is clear that there are a number of areas that can help you increase the value of your company. They are noted below. Although these will help you increase the value of your business, the most important element is to increase revenue, build cash flow and build an even better business model. We believe overall that you have a good business model today; it should just be leveraged further. Many companies we work with purchase another company to build their business value. Although it appears difficult initially, it tends to be the easiest method to build business value. With the current state of your business, you would be able to leverage your business model (i.e. put in your existing processes and systems) into another business that does not have your good traits. You would be able to benefit from another organization that has strengths that you might not yet possess. Similar to a Strategic buyer, you would be looking for a company that:

  - ○ Has better systems, controls and processes that you could leverage
  - ○ A facility that might allow you to balance your capacity constraints
  - ○ Has products that you could sell into your existing channels and vice versa
  - ○ Has revenues between $1-5 million (or larger depending on the opportunity)
  - ○ Enables you to purchase a management team, sales force and much more….

  From our understanding, the Industry is fairly fragmented with many small distributors. Therefore, finding another company that could provide you with the right elements you need to <u>increase the value of your business</u> and <u>make your business more attractive for purchase from a potential buyer</u> appears feasible. Given the right transaction structure this could be very lucrative for you.

- ○ *Evaluate your current pricing arrangements*

  Given our current economic times, this may sound rather crazy, but evaluate your current pricing arrangements to see if you can raise your prices in select areas. We understand that your business has been impacted by the current economic climate. We are not aware whether you receive the orders for the majority of your quotes (>90%) that you provide to your customers. If a large percentage is placed with your company, you should consider raising your prices to further improve cash flow. Especially if your customers have little basis of comparison

o *Standardize pricing to improve cash flow & gain tighter controls*
By standardizing the pricing, cash flow should improve. From our analysis, it appears that Fred processes about 57% of all orders and handles about 79% of all revenues. Fred's average margins are below Al's by approximately 3%, impacting the bottom line. Based on the above assumptions, by the standardizing prices, you should see an improvement of about $50-100,000 to the bottom line.

o *Do not establish a long-term lease.*
Work this out with a potential buyer so he/she has flexibility to secure the existing lease cost with you and/or move from the existing space.

o *Move XXXXX into more of a "CEO role"*
If a buyer views you functioning more as a CEO rather than being deeply embedded in the operations, processing orders on behalf of customers on a regular basis, he/she will see the opportunity to grow the business beyond the current state.

Role of the Business Owner

Value Creation

CEO – Strategic, business management

Breaking through the Barrier

Operational oversight, customer hand holding

Chief cook, bottle washer

Some of the reporting and analysis mentioned above in the "systems and controls" commentary (around the financial and operational reports) are fundamental elements that are required to function more as a CEO.

In our experience, we have seen that highly skilled entrepreneurs tend to get embedded into the company's operations as they develop strong relationships with their customers. The customers ask for the owner personally to handle the order and continue managing the relationship. We find that many business owners struggle to make the shift from a hands-on person to functioning more in an upper management role as a CEO.

o *Establish more formal financial reporting information and controls*
We would suggest having a clear set of financial reports that are generated on a periodic basis to manage the business. This would help you to move toward a CEO function, if you so chose.

o *Place the business on the web*

Today, many customers call the Company to get a price quote. This takes much time away from identifying and building new business. To ease this administrative burden, a system can be built for the customers to automatically:

- Request a quote
- Place an order
- Check inventory availability
- Check the order status

The system could be placed on the web allowing Sample to focus more on distribution and less so order taking. In addition, the company could automate the drop ship/subcontractor management process improving margins even further and tracking relevant data.

o *Begin expanding the integrated supplier arrangements to a regional/national basis*
The more that these arrangements are leveraged, the more competitors will be challenged. A buyer will view this as real value in the business, allowing him/her to truly compete on a larger scale with the larger players.

o *Begin distributing your customer base*
As noted above, about 50% of your business is done with the State. By distributing your customer base (not reducing it), you will be better positioned to whether unforeseen circumstances with any one large customer.

o *Begin building a sales force*
We are aware that you are not interested in building a sales force. Should the value not be attractive to sell, we would suggest that you further build your revenue base. Some options are:

- Hire a sales manager and establish sales targets
- Secure the MEMA contract. We are aware you are already attempting to secure this contract. By securing the MEMA contract with a "guaranteed" income stream you build the business with a stronger revenue base and stronger cash flows.

4. What could the value potentially increase to?

This is a **very difficult question to answer**. As you have read in the report, there are many elements that impact value. Given the industry's dynamics, financial position, operating efficiencies, etc. future results of a business are highly unpredictable. To provide a degree of context on this issue (in a **highly simplified manner**), the following outlines some preliminary financial projections. Based on these projections, we have estimated what value could be garnered. Please note this estimate **cannot be relied upon** as projections may or may not mirror actual results.

	Projected Current Yr.	Case 1	Case 2	Case 3	Case 4	Case 5
Target Revenues	5,500,000	6,000,000	7,000,000	8,000,000	9,000,000	10,000,000
Target % Cost of Sales *	76.6%	76.6%	76.6%	76.6%	76.6%	76.6%
Target $ Cost of Sales	4,214,444	4,597,575	5,363,838	6,130,100	6,896,363	7,662,626
Gross Profit	1,285,556	1,402,425	1,636,162	1,869,900	2,103,637	2,337,374
Target Net Expenses	600,000	650,000	700,000	750,000	800,000	850,000
Target Mgr/Owner Salary	120,000	125,000	150,000	175,000	200,000	225,000
Adjusted EBIT	565,556	627,425	786,162	944,900	1,103,637	1,262,374
Target Ratios:						
Gross Profit	23.4%	23.4%	23.4%	23.4%	23.4%	23.4%
Net Expenses	10.9%	10.8%	10.0%	8.8%	8.3%	8.0%
Adjusted EBIT	10.3%	10.5%	11.2%	11.8%	12.3%	12.6%
Estimates:						
Depreciation	15,000	15,000	15,000	30,000	30,000	40,000
Interest	5,000	5,000	10,000	25,000	30,000	30,000
EBITD	580,556	642,425	801,162	974,900	1,133,637	1,302,374
EBIT	565,556	627,425	786,162	944,900	1,103,637	1,262,374
EBITD	10.6%	10.7%	11.4%	12.2%	12.6%	13.0%
EBIT	10.3%	10.5%	11.2%	11.8%	12.3%	12.6%

* Period Average used in projections

Lets take one case, the $10 million dollar business. If you were able to grow your company to $10 million dollars (by acquiring another company, increasing the State business and/or landing the MEMA contract), what could be the potential value of the company? As you have seen in the calculations and worksheets above there are many methods to determine value. And as a result, the values can vary quite dramatically to command the highest price possible. To provide some perspective, lets use one method (the multiple EBIT method) to estimate value. Once again, this method may not be reflective of the method that will actually be used upon an eventual sale. Nor might it be reflective of the method that will attract the highest value possible.

	Type EBIT		Range of Multiple	Range of Value		
			4	5,049,498		
1)	Adjusted EBIT	1,262,374	5	6,311,872		
			6	7,574,247		
	Appropriate Multiple		5.5 *			
	Probable Adjusted EBIT Value				$	6,943,060
2)	EBITD		5	6,511,872		
		1,302,374	6	7,814,247		
			7	9,116,621		
	Appropriate Multiple		5.5 *			
	Probable EBITD Value				$	7,163,060
3)	EBIT		4	5,049,498		
		1,262,374	5	6,311,872		
			6	7,574,247		
			7	8,836,621		
	Appropriate Multiple		5.5 *			
	Probable EBIT Value				$	6,943,060

Summary of EBIT Values:		Weight		
EBIT-DA	6,943,060	2	13,886,119	
EBITD	7,163,060	2	14,326,119	
EBIT	6,943,060	1	6,943,060	
	21,049,179	5.00	35,155,298	

Straight Average	7,016,393		
	Weighted Average		7,031,060
	Probable EBIT Method Value	$	7,000,000

The method used has many assumptions built into it, none of which can be relied upon for future results. Based on case 5 above, the potential value might reach $7,000,000. One fundamental assumption used throughout this estimate is, given the size of a business, the business has the potential to attract a different multiple.

As noted in the industry overview section, the company currently falls into the $2-5M sales volume category. Companies that are among higher bandwidths of revenue and EBIT attract higher multiples. In order to attract a higher multiple, the business must move to a different level. Buyers view companies that have more revenues as more established with a lower risk attached to the business. This is one reason among many why a higher multiple might be offered for a business.

Sales Volume	# Co's (est.)	%
$100 Million+	3	0.1%
$50-100	10	0.5%
$25-50	11	0.6%
$10-25	60	3.1%
$5-10	110	5.6%
$2-5	270	13.8%
<$2 million	1,500	76.4%
Total	1,964	100.0%

5. **Should I place my business up for sale (a personal decision)?**
   The answer to this question is completely personal. As you are well aware (and you would never want another person to make this decision on your behalf) we cannot make this decision for you. The only guidance we can provide is the information that we have found that others use in their decision making criteria. Some questions that business owners typically ask themselves at this point in the process are:
   - o Given the potential risks identified from a buyer's perspective, do you (the business owner) feel it is a satisfactory price for the business?
   - o Will I be able to maintain a similar standard of living if I invest the net proceeds received from a potential sale (i.e. salary, benefits, etc.)?
   - o Do I have confidence (and energy) that I can build the business' value?
   - o Is there any risk that I am currently assuming by operating the business (e.g. changes in the industry, new regulations, loss of contracts, etc.) that might impact the future value?
   - o What will I do with my time if I decide to sell the business?
   - o Will my time and energy be best suited in this business or in another direction to meet my longer-term goals and objectives?
   - o What is the return on my effort (investment) over these years and will it increase over the next 5 years?

Ultimately, the decision is yours as to how you would like to proceed to build and secure your future net worth. We are happy to provide you with guidance as needed.

6. **In summary, what are my options to pursue?**
   To assist you in making a decision, we have outlined some of the options that might be available to you. These options are not intended to be comprehensive in nature but rather a simple summary of options with major logical next steps that you may or may not choose to pursue. These decisions are yours and solely yours. We will be happy to discuss them further with you to assist you with the process.

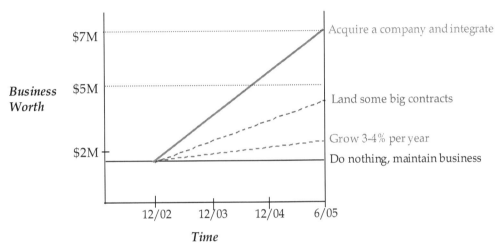

o *Do nothing. Leave everything as is (maintain the business).*
   You could do nothing with the business. You would probably want to evaluate the future potential to increase value. Another option could be to pursue a completely different business opportunity that would maximize your investment of time and effort while keeping this business in tact. This would complement your move into a CEO role, thereby further removing you from the operations and strategically building your net worth.

o *Do not sell the business. Build the value of the business further.*
   ▪ Evaluate if (and if so, when) you might want to sell the business
   ▪ Depending on your time frame, consider pursuing
      · Buying a competitor (acquire a company to integrate)
      · Hiring a sales force (grow 3-4% per year with the industry)
      · More aggressively selling into your larger accounts (land some big contracts)

These do not have to be done independently of each other, they can be done at the same time. If you pursue buying another company, you will have to:

- Develop a business profile of the type of business you might look to purchase
- Find and evaluate a business to purchase
- Develop a plan to increase the business's value

- *Sell the business for about $2,000,000*
  - Organize and prepare the facility for a potential sale
  - Develop an offering memorandum to present the business for sale
  - Gather the information that a buyer will look at during due diligence
  - Find and screen the "right" buyer
  - Present the business to prospective buyers
  - Negotiate the value and structure of the transaction

Glossary

Accounting policies	The principles, bases, conventions, rules and procedures adopted by management in preparing and presenting financial statements.
Accounting system	The principles, methods and procedures relating to the recording, classification, and reporting of the transactions of an entity. In most contexts, the term is synonymous with financial information system.
Acquisition debt service	The cost of monies borrowed to acquire the business.
Acquisition process	The basic stages of an acquisition are: • Strategy: developing a good strategy for strengthening the competitive capabilities of the existing business. • Planning: detailing a well-planned, team-based approach to making an acquisition. • Execution: executing the right type and amount of careful assessment and analysis. • Completion: completing the negotiations and closing the deal on favorable terms.
Adjusted EBIT	Pre-tax earnings plus owner's compensation, depreciation, amortization, interest and non recurring and discretionary expenses.
Agent/Agency	A person or company that has the authority to act on behalf of another (e.g., someone who makes an agreement on behalf of the Buyer).
Acquirer	The prospective buyer of a business or other asset.
Authorization to close	Written authorization by both buyer and seller to prepare closing documents.
Business valuation	The act of determining the value of, or the

estimated value of, a business enterprise or an interest therein.

Business Valuator A professional employed in the provision of business valuation and related services.

Buyer The prospective acquirer of a business or significant asset (e.g., plant or real estate).

Caveats A term used in this guidance to describe matters included in the engagement letter and/or our reports that help warn the client about the limitations of the due diligent engagement.

Competitive advantage The strategies, skills, knowledge, resources or competencies that differentiate a business from its competitors.

Conditions Situations subject to third party control , such as bank financing, or a list of actions that must be taken prior to closing.

Confidentiality agreement A legal document whereby the Buyer pledges to keep strictly confidential, and return on request, any and all information provided by the seller.

Contingency An existing condition, situation or set of circumstances involving uncertainty as to possible gain or loss to an entity that will be resolved when one or more future events occur or fail to occur.

Contingency removal Written satisfaction of a condition that must be met for a sale to be made.

Cost of goods Cost of goods purchased for resale.

Cost of sales Same as above plus the cost of labor to produce the product.

Counter offer Reply to an offer to purchase with

modifications to the original or last offer.

Covenants — A commitment made by the Buyer or Seller. For example, a commitment by the Seller that, subsequent to signing the purchase agreement but prior to closing, they will preserve the assets and continue to operate so that the business and goodwill being acquired will not diminish.

Culture — The beliefs, habits and behaviors of an entity. The culture of a business affects its ability to work in teams, to manage change, to innovate, etc. Culture is also reflected in management style and standards of customer service.

Deal breaker — A deal breaker is a significant issue relating to the proposed acquisition between the Buyer and the Vendor that needs to be resolved in order to close the deal.

Discretionary earnings — Earnings available for Debt Service, Owner's Compensation and actual Depreciation Reserves.

Divestiture team — A group of people formed by the Seller to manage the sale or divestiture of a company or division.

Due diligence — The process of systematically obtaining and assessing information in order to identify and contain the risks associated with buying a business.

Earn-out — A method of structuring a transaction whereby the ultimate purchase price is dependent in part on the future performance of the business being acquired.

EBIT — Earnings Before Interest and Taxes.

EBIT-D — Earnings Before Interest Taxes and

Depreciation

EBIT-DA   Earnings Before Interest Taxes
                               Depreciation and Amortization

Engagement letter   A letter that summarizes the terms of an
                               engagement.

F

Forecast   Future-oriented financial information
                               prepared using assumptions all of which
                               reflect the entity's planned courses of
                               action for the period covered given
                               management's judgement as to the most
                               probable set of economic conditions.

Fraud   Intentional misrepresentations of financial
                               statements by one or more individuals
                               among management, employees, or third
                               parties. Fraud may involve manipulation,
                               falsification or alteration of records or
                               documents, misappropriation of assets,
                               suppression or omission of the effects of
                               transactions from records or documents,
                               recording of transactions without
                               substance; or misapplication of accounting
                               standards.

G

Gross profit   Revenues or Income less cost of goods sold.

H   There are no glossary entries for this
                               letter.

I

Indemnification   A promise by one person to protect another
                               person from an anticipated or potential
                               loss. For example, a promise by the Seller
                               to assume certain potential future
                               liabilities (e.g., tax reassessments, product
                               or health and safety liabilities, etc.)
                               relating to past activities of the business.

Information package   A compilation of corporate information provided by the Seller to the Buyer in connection with the sale of a business. The Seller prepares the information or selling package to expose the business that is for sale to interested potential purchasers. Frequently, the target will prepare two separate packages - one which provides general information on what is being offered for sale and a second more detailed document made available to potential purchasers that have shown a serious interest in proceeding with the acquisition. Due to the sensitive nature of certain information such as markets, customers and financial information, the target will often only provide this information after the signing of the letter of intent. Furthermore, the client may only be given access to sensitive and confidential information through a staging process. Information packages are good sources of background information and may address the following:

- history of the company
- reasons for selling and opportunities for potential purchaser
- summary of products and/or services
- analysis of market, customer profile and competition
- description of current operations
- description of plant, property and equipment
- description of important suppliers
- analysis of human resources
- summary of financial information.

Information technology The expertise, facilities, processes, hardware, software and data available to assist in attaining business objectives.

Inspection Review records, documents, plant and facilities prior to transfer.

J There are no glossary entries for this letter.

K

There are no glossary entries for this letter.

L

Letter of intent

A document signifying genuine interest in reaching a final agreement, conditional upon the results of more detailed due diligence and negotiations, that may include:

- the issues or bases of understanding that have been agreed, in general terms
- the major issues that remain to be resolved
- agreed-upon procedures for going forward including the provision of more detailed information about the target by the Seller
- an indication that the letter of intent is not intended to represent a final binding agreement on the parties

Remembering that the Buyer has only completed an initial assessment at this point, the Buyer must be cautious about entering into any binding agreement or commitment on important issues before having obtained all the necessary information. It is vitally important that the Buyer obtain legal advice at this stage so that you understand precisely what commitments, if any, you are making.

M

Management

Management refers to the individuals in an entity that have the authority and the responsibility to manage the entity. The positions of these individuals, and their titles, vary from one entity to another and, to some extent, from one country to another depending on the local laws and customs. Thus, when the context requires it, the term includes the board of directors or committees of the board which are designated to oversee certain matters, (e.g., audit committee).

N

Non-competition agreement
An agreement which specifies the period of time during which a Seller or departing key employee cannot compete directly with the Buyer.

O

Offer
See letter of intent

P

Physical examination
Inspection of a tangible item, usually other than a document, such as an item of equipment.

Projection
Future-oriented financial information prepared using assumptions that reflect the entity's planned courses of action for the period covered given management's judgement as to the most probable set of economic conditions, together with one or more hypotheses that are assumptions which are consistent with the purpose of the information but are not necessarily the most probable in management's judgement.
Also see forecast, future-oriented financial information and "what if" scenarios.

Proforma financial information
The financial information that relates to events and actions that have not yet occurred and may not occur.

Purchase and sale agreement
This legal document records the final understanding of the parties with respect to the proposed transaction.

Q
There are no glossary entries for this letter.

R

Rate of return	Return on invested capital (calculated as a percentage). Often a Buyer has, as one of his investment criteria, a minimum acceptable rate of return on an acquisition.
Redundant assets	Assets which are not necessary for the ongoing operations of the business.
Related party	A person or entity that has the ability to control or exercise significant influence over the other party in making financial and operating decisions. Accordingly, subsidiaries, parent companies, sister companies and entities accounted for by the equity method are considered to be related parties, as are principal owners, members of boards of directors, management and members of their immediate families.
Related party transaction	A transfer of resources or obligations between related parties, regardless of whether or not a price is charged.
Representations	See Warranties.

S

Seller	The owner(s) of the entity being aquired.
Sunk costs	An unrecoverable cost resulting from an irreversible past decision.

T

Target	The business, or significant asset (e.g., plant or real estate) being considered for purchase by a Buyer from a Seller.
Trend analysis	An analytical procedure involving the analysis of the changes in a given account balance or class of transactions between the current and prior periods or over

several accounting periods.

U	There are no glossary entries for this letter.
V	There are no glossary entries for this letter.

W

Warranties	Statements made by the Seller with respect to certain elements of the proposed transaction (e.g., financial position of the business at closing date, level of sales achieved, collectibility of accounts receivable, extent of contingent liabilities, exposure to environmental issues, etc.) which, if proven to be untrue, may give the Buyer the right to make a claim for damages from the Seller.
"What if" scenarios	Analysis of the effect of possible future situations such as economic downturns, increased sales, changes in interest rates or price levels, new competitors or technologies, etc. See also forecast, future-oriented financial information and projection.
X	There are no glossary entries for this letter.
Y	There are no glossary entries for this letter.
Z	There are no glossary entries for this letter.

Exit Strategies

Many resources address making money. Few, if any, can show you how to create value and wealth with your business. This unique book and software combination is based upon *actual in the field experience and not pedantic theory*. The book gives you scores of proven methods and tips aimed at increasing the value of and creating wealth with your business.

Investigate a Business

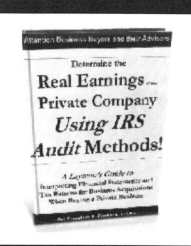

The real earnings are not found on the bottom line - they are hidden between the lines. Learn to use <u>Actual IRS Agents Audit Methods to Expose the Real Earnings of any Private business.</u> This Book and Software combination has been expressly created for the non-financial entrepreneur or executive engaged in buying or selling Private Companies.

Sell a Business

"How to Sell Your Business for the Most Money" (*without anyone knowing it's for sale*). The success rate of those selling, or buying, Private businesses does not present a pretty picture. Most all who attempt it fail, <u>even the professionals</u>! This book and software combo will help you avoid the mistakes and traps that catch the typical business seller.

Broker Businesses

This New Book and Software Package Provides Step by Step Instructions detailing How to Become the Best Business Broker in Town or *How to sell essentially every listing you take (9+ of 10)* Created especially for Business Brokers, and others Selling Businesses

Business Transfer Documentation

Book of Samples plus CD - Transaction documentation - All the documents needed to Buy, Sell or Merge a Private company are on this easy to use CD. Find the "just right" document quickly and easily. Added Bonus - hundreds of contingency and special wording to address any situation that may arise.

Business Valuation

Reveals the previously unwritten rules for Transaction Valuations of private businesses. *The book explains and the software calculates the impact that limited or restrictive financing has on value and transaction structure.* Calculate the right price and terms for any private businesses sale.

Buy a Business

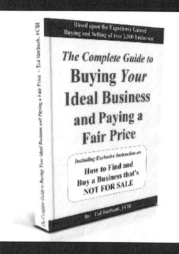

This practical guide, written in understandable "shirt sleeve" language, simplifies a very complex subject. The book focuses upon the motivations and perceptions that drive a sale and the software "crunches the numbers." Case studies and examples are provided to illustrate every major point.

Comprehensive Packages

Business Broker's Selling System - for business brokers
How can our *Business Selling* System methods be so superior to those employed by the majority of business brokers and essentially all Business Brokerage Franchisors? This nine part book and software package reveals the secrets to being able to sell essentially every listing you take.

Wealth Creation and Business Selling System - for business owners and their advisors
Scores of resources are available to help small businesses become more profitable but virtually none on how to make a small business more valuable. This eight part book and software combo will show you how to use Public company wealth creation techniques to build extraordinary wealth in your family businesses

Business Buying System - for business buyers
How to determine the business that's just right for you. Then, how to find it and buy it even if it's not for sale! Profit from the experience and insight gained in negotiating more than two thousand business transfers. This practical six part guide, written in understandable "shirt sleeve" language, simplifies a very complex subject. The book focuses upon the motivations and perceptions that drive a sale and the software "crunches the numbers." Case studies and examples are provided to illustrate every major point.

Books and Software from Parker-Nelson Publishing – for more information go to

BuySellBiz.com

Made in the USA
Charleston, SC
24 April 2012